D1583006

WITHDRAWN

Library Learning Information

To renew this item call:

0115 929 3388
or visit
www.ideastore.co.uk

TOWER HAMLETS

Created and managed by Tower Hamlets Council

A TED HUGHES BESTIARY

A TED HUGHES BESTIARY

POEMS

selected by

Alice Oswald

FABER & FABER

First published in 2014
by Faber & Faber Ltd
Bloomsbury House
74–77 Great Russell Street
London WC1B 3DA

Typeset by Faber & Faber Ltd
Printed in England by Martins the Printers, Berwick-upon-Tweed

All rights reserved
© The Estate of Ted Hughes, 2014
Introduction and selection © Alice Oswald, 2014

The right of The Estate of Ted Hughes to be identified as author of this work
has been asserted in accordance with Section 77 of the
Copyright, Designs and Patents Act 1988

A CIP record for this book
is available from the British Library

ISBN 978–0–571–30143–0

MIX
Paper from
responsible sources
FSC® C013254
www.fsc.org

TOWER HAMLETS
LIBRARIES

91000004479838	
Bertrams	18/09/2014
821.914	£14.99
THISCH	TH14000596

WITHDRAWN

2 4 6 8 10 9 7 5 3 1

Acknowledgements

I'm grateful to Carol Hughes and Paul Keegan for their help in assembling this book and to Martha Sprackland for overseeing its production.

Contents

Introduction

Ted Hughes said, in *Poetry in the Making*, that he thought of his poems as animals, meaning that he wanted them to have 'a vivid life of their own'. So there is something very distilled and self-defining about his animal poems, almost as if they were prayers to language itself; which is why, out of the mass of his *Collected Poems*, it has seemed a good idea to gather this *Bestiary*.

A bestiary was originally a Christian idea – a book of animals sketchily recorded and then reduced to emblems – which sounds inimical to Hughes, whose animals are so radiantly themselves. The purpose of a bestiary (and this purpose was more and more neurotically observed through the Middle Ages) was to find distinctions between Man and the animals; but Hughes always worked in the opposite direction, aiming to show us what they have in common. He was wary of any project that was too narrowly Christian.

Nevertheless, there is some bestiary flavour – half scientific, half imaginative – in the tone of Hughes's voice. He writes, in the notes to *Moortown Diary*, about his practice of 'getting reasonably close to what is going on, and staying close, and of excluding everything else that might be pressing to interfere with the watching eye'; but then also, in a letter to his brother, he finds fault with the watching eye: 'when a man becomes a mirror, he just ceases to be interesting to men.'

His poems, from one collection to the next, oscillate between these extremes. Sometimes – for example in *Moortown Diary*, *Remains of Elmet*, *Birthday Letters* – they catch the 'vivid life' of their subject by standing back, turning down the voice, letting the facts in all their strangeness bend the verse. Sometimes – for example in *Crow* or *Cave Birds* – the language comes out tensed and singing, as if by dictation from the Underworld. I've tried to do justice to that doubleness. Like a bestiary, this book is a herd of both outward and inward animals, but, unlike a bestiary, there is nothing moralising about its vision.

What is it that turns language into an animal? What gives poems a 'vivid life' of their own, such that 'nothing can be added to them or taken away without maiming and perhaps even killing them'? I think, in Hughes's case, it's a matter of percussion. There is something irresistible about the rhythm of a Hughes poem, which makes every word of it connected and essential.

> The lark begins to go up
> Like a warning
> As if the globe were uneasy –
>
> Barrel-chested for heights,
> Like an Indian of the high Andes,
>
> A whippet head, barbed like a hunting arrow,
>
> But leaden
> With muscle
> For the struggle
> Against
> Earth's centre.
>
> And leaden
> For ballast
> In the rocketing storms of the breath.
>
> Leaden
> Like a bullet
> To supplant
> Life from its centre.
>
> ('Skylarks')

These are ecstatic sounds, not so much spoken as drummed. They remind me of accounts of ancient dancers, who could disorder their minds and turn into any creature or character by means of music. It's as if the bodily movement of Hughes's verse is actually driving him through the shape of a skylark.

The rule of this selection is that the poems included, like the one just quoted, should embody animals, not just describe them, which is why so many of Hughes's children's poems, with their ironic, chatting rhythms, have been omitted. On the other hand, I've allowed some poems, such as 'The Lake' and 'Thistles', because, although not strictly speaking animal, they become so in the process of the writing; and, in keeping with the bestiary tradition, I've put in plenty of imaginary animals: Wodwo, the Lovepet, Littleblood, the Human Calf, the Phoenix. I've aimed to keep a balance between the different books and styles, but perhaps I've favoured those poems that have the wildest tunes.

The poems are arranged chronologically, because my focus is not really on Hughes as 'animal poet' or 'eco-poet', in spite of his obvious and lifelong commitment to the natural world. I'm more interested in presenting his work dramatically as a pursuit or flight. I picture him, like Taliesin, engaged in a kind of folktale chase, hiding himself in different animal forms: from the Hawk to the Fox to the Bull to the Rat to the Crow, ending with that strange final creature, the Prophet:

> Crazed by my soul's thirst
> Through a dark land I staggered.
> And a six-winged seraph
> Halted me at a crossroads.
> With fingers of dream
> He touched my eye-pupils.

My eyes, prophetic, recoiled
Like a startled eaglet's.

('The Prophet')

This poem, a translation from Pushkin and one of the last pieces he wrote, might seem an odd choice for a book of animals, but its position at the end, completing the poet's story, puts the rest into perspective. You do get the feeling, when you read his letters, that he lived life on this dreamed or nightmare level.

Hughes was quite clear about the importance of folktale in balancing the imagination; and quite clear about the role of imagination in balancing our impact on the earth. 'What alters the imagination', he said, 'alters everything.' My hope is that this anthology will alter people's imaginations. When I was compiling it, I had to type the poems to work out which ones to discard. About two weeks through the task, I noticed an unusual brightness behind my eyes. It was as if the top of my skull had been wedged open and the poems were moving around in there like animals woken by daylight. Although the poems are here assembled and printed in a book, I challenge the reader to imagine them still unbound – like the Thought-Fox – 'Brilliantly, concentratedly, / Coming about [their] own business'.

ALICE OSWALD

Four prose excerpts

There are all sorts of ways of capturing animals and birds and fish. I spent most of my time, up to the age of fifteen or so, trying out many of these ways and when my enthusiasm began to wane, as it did gradually, I started to write poems. You might not think that these two interests, capturing animals and writing poems, have much in common. But the more I think back the more sure I am that with me the two interests have been one interest. My pursuit of mice at threshing time when I was a boy, snatching them from under the sheaves as the sheaves were lifted away out of the stack and popping them into my pocket till I had thirty or forty crawling around in the lining of my coat, that and my present pursuit of poems seem to me to be different stages of the same fever. In a way, I suppose, I think of poems as a sort of animal. They have their own life, like animals, by which I mean that they seem quite separate from any person, even from their author, and nothing can be added to them or taken away without maiming and perhaps even killing them. And they have a certain wisdom. They know something special . . . something perhaps which we are very curious to learn. Maybe my concern has been to capture not animals particularly and not poems, but simply things which have a vivid life of their own outside mine.

(Poetry in the Making, 1967)

[xvii]

*

The luminous spirit (maybe he is a crowd of spirits), that takes account of everything and gives everything its meaning, is missing, not missing, just incommunicado. But here and there, it may be, we hear it.

It is human of course, but it is also everything that lives. When we hear it, we understand what a strange creature is living in this Universe, and somewhere at the core of us – strange, beautiful, pathetic, terrible. Some animals and birds express this being pure and without effort, and then you hear the whole desolate, final reality in a voice, a tone.

(*Orghast*, 1971)

*

Both Hawk and Pike (like the Bull) are motionless, or almost
motionless. In a planned, straightforward way, I began them
as a series in which they would be angels – hanging in the
radiant glory around the creator's throne, composed of terrific,
holy power (there's a line in 'Hawk Roosting' almost verbatim
from Job), but either quite still, or moving only very slowly –
at peace, and actually composed of the glowing substance of
the law. Like Sons of God. Pike (luce = 'fish of light'), Apis Bull
and Horus. I wanted to focus my natural world – these
familiars of my boyhood – in a 'divine' dimension. I wanted to
express my sense of that. Again, these creatures are 'at rest in
the law' – obedient, law-abiding, and are as I say the law in
creaturely form. If the Hawk and the Pike kill, they kill within
the law and their killing is a sacrament in this sense. It is an act
not of violence but of law.

(*Poetry and Violence*, 1971)

*

I was aware, as I went on writing, that above all I wanted to rid my language of the penumbra of abstractions that to my way of thinking cluttered the writing of all other poetry being written by post-Auden poets . . . So I squirmed and weaseled a way towards a language that would be wholly my own. Not my own by being exotic or eccentric in some way characteristic of me. But my own in that it would be an ABC of the simplest terms that I could feel rooted into my own life, my own feelings about quite definite things. So this conscious search for a 'solid' irrefutably defined basic (and therefore 'limited') kit of words drew me inevitably towards the solid irrefutably defined basic kit of my experiences – drew me towards animals, basically: my childhood and adolescent pantheon of wild creatures, which were saturated by first hand intense feeling that went back to my infancy. Those particular subjects, in a sense, were the models on which I fashioned my workable language.

(Letter to Anne-Lorraine Bijou, 1992)

A TED HUGHES BESTIARY

The Hawk in the Rain

I drown in the drumming ploughland, I drag up
Heel after heel from the swallowing of the earth's mouth,
From clay that clutches my each step to the ankle
With the habit of the dogged grave, but the hawk

Effortlessly at height hangs his still eye.
His wings hold all creation in a weightless quiet,
Steady as a hallucination in the streaming air.
While banging wind kills these stubborn hedges,

Thumbs my eyes, throws my breath, tackles my heart,
And rain hacks my head to the bone, the hawk hangs
The diamond point of will that polestars
The sea drowner's endurance: and I,

Bloodily grabbed dazed last-moment-counting
Morsel in the earth's mouth, strain towards the master-
Fulcrum of violence where the hawk hangs still.
That maybe in his own time meets the weather

Coming the wrong way, suffers the air, hurled upside down,
Fall from his eye, the ponderous shires crash on him,
The horizon trap him; the round angelic eye
Smashed, mix his heart's blood with the mire of the land.

The Jaguar

The apes yawn and adore their fleas in the sun.
The parrots shriek as if they were on fire, or strut
Like cheap tarts to attract the stroller with the nut.
Fatigued with indolence, tiger and lion

Lie still as the sun. The boa-constrictor's coil
Is a fossil. Cage after cage seems empty, or
Stinks of sleepers from the breathing straw.
It might be painted on a nursery wall.

But who runs like the rest past these arrives
At a cage where the crowd stands, stares, mesmerized,
As a child at a dream, at a jaguar hurrying enraged
Through prison darkness after the drills of his eyes

On a short fierce fuse. Not in boredom –
The eye satisfied to be blind in fire,
By the bang of blood in the brain deaf the ear –
He spins from the bars, but there's no cage to him

More than to the visionary his cell:
His stride is wildernesses of freedom:
The world rolls under the long thrust of his heel.
Over the cage floor the horizons come.

The Thought-Fox

I imagine this midnight moment's forest:
Something else is alive
Beside the clock's loneliness
And this blank page where my fingers move.

Through the window I see no star:
Something more near
Though deeper within darkness
Is entering the loneliness:

Cold, delicately as the dark snow,
A fox's nose touches twig, leaf;
Two eyes serve a movement, that now
And again now, and now, and now

Sets neat prints into the snow
Between trees, and warily a lame
Shadow lags by stump and in hollow
Of a body that is bold to come

Across clearings, an eye,
A widening deepening greenness,
Brilliantly, concentratedly,
Coming about its own business

Till, with a sudden sharp hot stink of fox
It enters the dark hole of the head.
The window is starless still; the clock ticks,
The page is printed.

The Horses

I climbed through woods in the hour-before-dawn dark.
Evil air, a frost-making stillness,

Not a leaf, not a bird –
A world cast in frost. I came out above the wood

Where my breath left tortuous statues in the iron light.
But the valleys were draining the darkness

Till the moorline – blackening dregs of the brightening
    grey –
Halved the sky ahead. And I saw the horses:

Huge in the dense grey – ten together –
Megalith-still. They breathed, making no move,

With draped manes and tilted hind-hooves,
Making no sound.

I passed: not one snorted or jerked its head.
Grey silent fragments

Of a grey silent world.

I listened in emptiness on the moor-ridge.
The curlew's tear turned its edge on the silence.

Slowly detail leafed from the darkness. Then the sun
Orange, red, red erupted

Silently, and splitting to its core tore and flung cloud,
Shook the gulf open, showed blue,

And the big planets hanging,
I turned

Stumbling in the fever of a dream, down towards
The dark woods, from the kindling tops,

And came to the horses.
                    There, still they stood,
But now steaming and glistening under the flow of light,

Their draped stone manes, their tilted hind-hooves
Stirring under a thaw while all around them

The frost showed its fires. But still they made no sound.
Not one snorted or stamped,

Their hung heads patient as the horizons,
High over valleys, in the red levelling rays –

In din of the crowded streets, going among the years, the faces,
May I still meet my memory in so lonely a place

Between the streams and the red clouds, hearing curlews,
Hearing the horizons endure.

Meeting

He smiles in a mirror, shrinking the whole
Sun-swung zodiac of light to a trinket shape
On the rise of his eye: it is a role

In which he can fling a cape,
And outloom life like Faustus. But once when
On an empty mountain slope

A black goat clattered and ran
Towards him, and set forefeet firm on a rock
Above and looked down

A square-pupilled yellow-eyed look
The black devil head against the blue air,
What gigantic fingers took

Him up and on a bare
Palm turned him close under an eye
That was like a living hanging hemisphere

And watched his blood's gleam with a ray
Slow and cold and ferocious as a star
Till the goat clattered away.

February

The wolf with its belly stitched full of big pebbles;
Nibelung wolves barbed like black pineforest
Against a red sky, over blue snow; or that long grin
Above the tucked coverlet – none suffice.

A photograph: the hairless, knuckled feet
Of the last wolf killed in Britain spoiled him for wolves:
The worst since has been so much mere Alsatian.
Now it is the dream cries 'Wolf!' where these feet

Print the moonlit doorstep, or run and run
Through the hush of parkland, bodiless, headless;
With small seeming of inconvenience
By day, too, pursue, siege all thought;

Bring him to an abrupt poring stop
Over engravings of gibbet-hung wolves,
As at a cage where the scraggy Spanish wolf
Danced, smiling, brown eyes doggily begging

A ball to be thrown. These feet, deprived,
Disdaining all that are caged, or storied, or pictured,
Through and throughout the true world search
For their vanished head, for the world

Vanished with the head, the teeth, the quick eyes –
Now, lest they choose his head,
Under severe moons he sits making
Wolf-masks, mouths clamped well onto the world.

Esther's Tomcat

Daylong this tomcat lies stretched flat
As an old rough mat, no mouth and no eyes.
Continual wars and wives are what
Have tattered his ears and battered his head.

Like a bundle of old rope and iron
Sleeps till blue dusk. Then reappear
His eyes, green as ringstones: he yawns wide red,
Fangs fine as a lady's needle and bright.

A tomcat sprang at a mounted knight,
Locked round his neck like a trap of hooks
While the knight rode fighting its clawing and bite.
After hundreds of years the stain's there

On the stone where he fell, dead of the tom:
That was at Barnborough. The tomcat still
Grallochs odd dogs on the quiet,
Will take the head clean off your simple pullet,

Is unkillable. From the dog's fury,
From gunshot fired point-blank he brings
His skin whole, and whole
From owlish moons of bekittenings

Among ashcans. He leaps and lightly
Walks upon sleep, his mind on the moon.
Nightly over the round world of men,
Over the roofs go his eyes and outcry.

Hawk Roosting

I sit in the top of the wood, my eyes closed.
Inaction, no falsifying dream
Between my hooked head and hooked feet:
Or in sleep rehearse perfect kills and eat.

The convenience of the high trees!
The air's buoyancy and the sun's ray
Are of advantage to me;
And the earth's face upward for my inspection.

My feet are locked upon the rough bark.
It took the whole of Creation
To produce my foot, my each feather:
Now I hold Creation in my foot

Or fly up, and revolve it all slowly –
I kill where I please because it is all mine.
There is no sophistry in my body:
My manners are tearing off heads –

The allotment of death.
For the one path of my flight is direct
Through the bones of the living.
No arguments assert my right:

The sun is behind me.
Nothing has changed since I began.
My eye has permitted no change.
I am going to keep things like this.

The Bull Moses

A hoist up and I could lean over
The upper edge of the high half-door,
My left foot ledged on the hinge, and look in at the byre's
Blaze of darkness: a sudden shut-eyed look
Backward into the head.
                    Blackness is depth
Beyond star. But the warm weight of his breathing,
The ammoniac reek of his litter, the hotly-tongued
Mash of his cud, steamed against me.
Then, slowly, as onto the mind's eye –
The brow like masonry, the deep-keeled neck:
Something come up there onto the brink of the gulf,
Hadn't heard of the world, too deep in itself to be called to,
Stood in sleep. He would swing his muzzle at a fly
But the square of sky where I hung, shouting, waving,
Was nothing to him; nothing of our light
Found any reflection in him.
                    Each dusk the farmer led him
Down to the pond to drink and smell the air,
And he took no pace but the farmer
Led him to take it, as if he knew nothing
Of the ages and continents of his fathers,
Shut, while he wombed, to a dark shed
And steps between his door and the duckpond;
The weight of the sun and the moon and the world
    hammered
To a ring of brass through his nostrils.
                    He would raise
His streaming muzzle and look out over the meadows,
But the grasses whispered nothing awake, the fetch

Of the distance drew nothing to momentum
In the locked black of his powers. He came strolling
    gently back,
Paused neither toward the pig-pens on his right,
Nor toward the cow-byres on his left: something
Deliberate in his leisure, some beheld future
Founding in his quiet.
                    I kept the door wide,
Closed it after him and pushed the bolt.

View of a Pig

The pig lay on a barrow dead.
It weighed, they said, as much as three men.
Its eyes closed, pink white eyelashes.
Its trotters stuck straight out.

Such weight and thick pink bulk
Set in death seemed not just dead.
It was less than lifeless, further off.
It was like a sack of wheat.

I thumped it without feeling remorse.
One feels guilty insulting the dead,
Walking on graves. But this pig
Did not seem able to accuse.

It was too dead. Just so much
A poundage of lard and pork.
Its last dignity had entirely gone.
It was not a figure of fun.

Too dead now to pity.
To remember its life, din, stronghold
Of earthly pleasure as it had been,
Seemed a false effort, and off the point.

Too deadly factual. Its weight
Oppressed me – how could it be moved?
And the trouble of cutting it up!
The gash in its throat was shocking, but not pathetic.

Once I ran at a fair in the noise
To catch a greased piglet
That was faster and nimbler than a cat,
Its squeal was the rending of metal.

Pigs must have hot blood, they feel like ovens.
Their bite is worse than a horse's –
They chop a half-moon clean out.
They eat cinders, dead cats.

Distinctions and admirations such
As this one was long finished with.
I stared at it a long time. They were going to scald it,
Scald it and scour it like a doorstep.

An Otter

Underwater eyes, an eel's
Oil of water body, neither fish nor beast is the otter:
　　Four-legged yet water-gifted, to outfish fish;
　　　　With webbed feet and long ruddering tail
　　　　And a round head like an old tomcat.

　　Brings the legend of himself
From before wars or burials, in spite of hounds and
　　　　vermin-poles;
　　Does not take root like the badger. Wanders, cries;
　　　　Gallops along land he no longer belongs to;
　　　　Re-enters the water by melting.

　　Of neither water nor land. Seeking
Some world lost when first he dived, that he cannot
　　　　come at since,
　　Takes his changed body into the holes of lakes;
　　　　As if blind, cleaves the stream's push till he licks
　　　　The pebbles of the source; from sea

　　To sea crosses in three nights
Like a king in hiding. Crying to the old shape of the
　　　　starlit land,
　　Over sunken farms where the bats go round,
　　　　Without answer. Till light and birdsong come
　　　　Walloping up roads with the milk wagon.

The hunt's lost him. Pads on mud,
Among sedges, nostrils a surface bead,
The otter remains, hours. The air,
Circling the globe, tainted and necessary,

Mingling tobacco-smoke, hounds and parsley,
Comes carefully to the sunk lungs.
So the self under the eye lies,
Attendant and withdrawn. The otter belongs

In double robbery and concealment –
From water that nourishes and drowns, and from land
That gave him his length and the mouth of the hound.
He keeps fat in the limpid integument

Reflections live on. The heart beats thick,
Big trout muscle out of the dead cold;
Blood is the belly of logic; he will lick
The fishbone bare. And can take stolen hold

On a bitch otter in a field full
Of nervous horses, but linger nowhere.
Yanked above hounds, reverts to nothing at all,
To this long pelt over the back of a chair.

Thrushes

Terrifying are the attent sleek thrushes on the lawn,
More coiled steel than living – a poised
Dark deadly eye, those delicate legs
Triggered to stirrings beyond sense – with a start, a bounce,
    a stab
Overtake the instant and drag out some writhing thing.
No indolent procrastinations and no yawning stares.
No sighs or head-scratchings. Nothing but bounce and stab
And a ravening second.

Is it their single-mind-sized skulls, or a trained
Body, or genius, or a nestful of brats
Gives their days this bullet and automatic
Purpose? Mozart's brain had it, and the shark's mouth
That hungers down the blood-smell even to a leak of its own
Side and devouring of itself: efficiency which
Strikes too streamlined for any doubt to pluck at it
Or obstruction deflect.

With a man it is otherwise. Heroisms on horseback,
Outstripping his desk-diary at a broad desk,
Carving at a tiny ivory ornament
For years: his act worships itself – while for him,
Though he bends to be blent in the prayer, how loud and
    above what
Furious spaces of fire do the distracting devils
Orgy and hosannah, under what wilderness
Of black silent waters weep.

Pike

Pike, three inches long, perfect
Pike in all parts, green tigering the gold.
Killers from the egg: the malevolent aged grin.
They dance on the surface among the flies.

Or move, stunned by their own grandeur
Over a bed of emerald, silhouette
Of submarine delicacy and horror.
A hundred feet long in their world.

In ponds, under the heat-struck lily pads –
Gloom of their stillness:
Logged on last year's black leaves, watching upwards.
Or hung in an amber cavern of weeds

The jaws' hooked clamp and fangs
Not to be changed at this date;
A life subdued to its instrument;
The gills kneading quietly, and the pectorals.

Three we kept behind glass,
Jungled in weed: three inches, four,
And four and a half: fed fry to them –
Suddenly there were two. Finally one.

With a sag belly and the grin it was born with.
And indeed they spare nobody.
Two, six pounds each, over two feet long,
High and dry and dead in the willow-herb –

One jammed past its gills down the other's gullet:
The outside eye stared: as a vice locks –
The same iron in this eye
Though its film shrank in death.

A pond I fished, fifty yards across,
Whose lilies and muscular tench
Had outlasted every visible stone
Of the monastery that planted them –

Stilled legendary depth:
It was as deep as England. It held
Pike too immense to stir, so immense and old
That past nightfall I dared not cast

But silently cast and fished
With the hair frozen on my head
For what might move, for what eye might move.
The still splashes on the dark pond,

Owls hushing the floating woods
Frail on my ear against the dream
Darkness beneath night's darkness had freed,
That rose slowly towards me, watching.

Stealing Trout on a May Morning

I park the car half in the ditch and switch off and sit.
The hot astonishment of my engine's arrival
Sinks through 5 a.m. silence and frost.
At the end of a long gash
An atrocity through the lace of first light
I sit with the reeking instrument.
I am on delicate business.
I want the steel to be cold instantly
And myself secreted three fields away
And the farms, back under their blankets, supposing a
    plane passed.

Because this is no wilderness you can just rip into.
Every leaf is plump and well-married,
Every grain of soil of known lineage, well-connected.
And the gardens are like brides fallen asleep
Before their weddings have properly begun.
The orchards are the hushed maids, fresh from convent . . .
It is too hushed, something improper is going to happen.
It is too ghostly proper, all sorts of liveried listenings
Tiptoe along the lanes and peer over hedges.

I listen for the eyes jerked open on pillows,
Their dreams washed with sudden ugly petroleum.
They need only look out at a sheep.
Every sheep within two miles
Is nailing me accurately down
With its hellishly-shaven starved-priest expression.

I emerge. The air, after all, has forgotten everything.
The sugared spindles and wings of grass
Are etched on great goblets. A pigeon falls into space.

The earth is coming quietly and darkly up from a
     great depth,
Still under the surface. I am unknown,
But nothing is surprised. The tarmac of the road
Is velvet with sleep, the hills are out cold.
A new earth still in its wrappers
Of gauze and cellophane,
The frost from the storage still on its edges,
My privilege to poke and sniff.
The sheep are not much more than the primroses.
And the river there, amazed with itself,
Flexing and trying its lights
And unused fish, that are rising
And sinking for the sheer novelty
As the sun melts the hill's spine and the spilled light
Flows through their gills . . .

My mind sinks, rising and sinking.
And the opening arms of the sky forget me
Into the buried tunnel of hazels. There
My boot dangles down, till a thing black and sudden
Savages it, and the river is heaping under,
Alive and malevolent,
A coiling glider of shock, the space-black
Draining off the night-moor, under the hazels . . .
But I drop and stand square in it, against it,
Then it is river again, washing its soul,
Its stones, its weeds, its fish, its gravels
And the rooty mouths of the hazels clear
Of the discolourings bled in
Off ploughlands and lanes . . .

At first, I can hardly look at it –
The riding tables, the corrugated

Shanty roofs tightening
To braids, boilings where boulders throw up
Gestures of explosion, black splitting everywhere
To drowning skirts of whiteness, a slither of mirrors
Under the wading hazels. Here it is shallow,
Ropes my knees, lobbing fake boomerangs,
A drowned woman loving each ankle,
But I'm heavier and I wade with them upstream,
Flashing my blue minnow
Up the open throats of water
And across through the side of the rush
Of alligator escaping along there
Under the beards of the hazels, and I slice
The wild nape-hair off the bald bulges,
Till the tightrope of my first footholds
Tangles away downstream
And my bootsoles move as to magnets.

Soon I deepen. And now I meet the piling mob
Of voices and hurriers coming towards me
And tumbling past me. I press through a panic . . .
This headlong river is a rout
Of tumbrils and gun-carriages, rags and metal,
All the funeral woe-drag of some overnight disaster
Mixed with planets, electrical storms and darkness
On a mapless moorland of granite,
Trailing past me with all its frights, its eyes
With what they have seen and still see,
They drag the flag off my head, a dark insistence
Tearing the spirits from my mind's edge and from
    under . . .

To yank me clear takes the sudden, strong spine
Of one of the river's real members –
Thoroughly made of dew, lightning and granite

Very slowly over four years. A trout, a foot long,
Lifting its head in a shawl of water,
Fins banked stiff like a trireme
It forces the final curve wide, getting
A long look at me. So much for the horror
It has changed places.
                    Now I am a man in a painting
(Under the mangy, stuffed head of a fox)
Painted about 1905
Where the river steams and the frost relaxes
On the pear-blossoms. The brassy wood-pigeons
Bubble their colourful voices, and the sun
Rises upon a world well-tried and old.

The Lake

Better disguised than the leaf-insect,

A sort of subtler armadillo,
The lake turns with me as I walk.

Snuffles at my feet for what I might drop or kick up,
Sucks and slobbers the stones, snorts through its lips

Into broken glass, smacks its chops.
It has eaten several my size

Without developing a preference –
Prompt, with a splash, to whatever I offer.

It ruffles in its wallow, or lies sunning,
Digesting old senseless bicycles

And a few shoes. The fish down there
Do not know they have been swallowed

Any more than the girl out there, who over the stern of
    a rowboat
Tests its depth with her reflection.

Yet how the outlet fears it!
                    – dragging it out,
Black and yellow, a maniac eel,

Battering it to death with sticks and stones.

Thistles

Against the rubber tongues of cows and the hoeing hands
    of men
Thistles spike the summer air
Or crackle open under a blue-black pressure.

Every one a revengeful burst
Of resurrection, a grasped fistful
Of splintered weapons and Icelandic frost thrust up

From the underground stain of a decayed Viking.
They are like pale hair and the gutturals of dialects.
Every one manages a plume of blood.

Then they grow grey, like men.
Mown down, it is a feud. Their sons appear,
Stiff with weapons, fighting back over the same ground.

Ghost Crabs

At nightfall, as the sea darkens,
A depth darkness thickens, mustering from the gulfs and the
    submarine badlands,
To the sea's edge. To begin with
It looks like rocks uncovering, mangling their pallor.
Gradually the labouring of the tide
Falls back from its productions,
Its power slips back from glistening nacelles, and they are crabs.
Giant crabs, under flat skulls, staring inland
Like a packed trench of helmets.
Ghosts, they are ghost-crabs.
They emerge
An invisible disgorging of the sea's cold
Over the man who strolls along the sands.
They spill inland, into the smoking purple
Of our woods and towns – a bristling surge
Of tall and staggering spectres
Gliding like shocks through water.
Our walls, our bodies, are no problem to them.
Their hungers are homing elsewhere.
We cannot see them or turn our minds from them.
Their bubbling mouths, their eyes
In a slow mineral fury
Press through our nothingness where we sprawl on beds,
Or sit in rooms. Our dreams are ruffled maybe,
Or we jerk awake to the world of possessions
With a gasp, in a sweat burst, brains jamming blind
Into the bulb-light. Sometimes, for minutes, a sliding
Staring
Thickness of silence

Presses between us. These crabs own this world.
All night, around us or through us,
They stalk each other, they fasten on to each other,
They mount each other, they tear each other to pieces,
They utterly exhaust each other.
They are the powers of this world.
We are their bacteria,
Dying their lives and living their deaths.
At dawn, they sidle back under the sea's edge.
They are the turmoil of history, the convulsion
In the roots of blood, in the cycles of concurrence.
To them, our cluttered countries are empty battleground.
All day they recuperate under the sea.
Their singing is like a thin sea-wind flexing in the rocks
    of a headland,
Where only crabs listen.

They are God's only toys.

Second Glance at a Jaguar

Skinful of bowls he bowls them,
The hip going in and out of joint, dropping the spine
With the urgency of his hurry
Like a cat going along under thrown stones, under cover,
Glancing sideways, running
Under his spine. A terrible, stump-legged waddle
Like a thick Aztec disemboweller,
Club-swinging, trying to grind some square
Socket between his hind legs round,
Carrying his head like a brazier of spilling embers,
And the black bit of his mouth, he takes it
Between his back teeth, he has to wear his skin out,
He swipes a lap at the water-trough as he turns,
Swivelling the ball of his heel on the polished spot,
Showing his belly like a butterfly.
At every stride he has to turn a corner
In himself and correct it. His head
Is like the worn down stump of another whole jaguar,
His body is just the engine shoving it forward,
Lifting the air up and shoving on under,
The weight of his fangs hanging the mouth open,
Bottom jaw combing the ground. A gorged look,
Gangster, club-tail lumped along behind gracelessly,
He's wearing himself to heavy ovals,
Muttering some mantra, some drum-song of murder
To keep his rage brightening, making his skin
Intolerable, spurred by the rosettes, the Cain-brands,
Wearing the spots off from the inside,
Rounding some revenge. Going like a prayer-wheel,
The head dragging forward, the body keeping up,

The hind legs lagging. He coils, he flourishes
The blackjack tail as if looking for a target,
Hurrying through the underworld, soundless.

Song of a Rat

The rat is in the trap, it is in the trap,
And attacking heaven and earth with a mouthful of screeches
  like torn tin,

An effective gag.
When it stops screeching, it pants

And cannot think
'This has no face, it must be God' or

'No answer is also an answer.'
Iron jaws, strong as the whole earth

Are stealing its backbone
For a crumpling of the Universe with screechings,

For supplanting every human brain inside its skull with a
  rat-body that knots and unknots,
A rat that goes on screeching,

Trying to uproot itself into each escaping screech,
But its long fangs bar that exit –

The incisors bared to the night spaces, threatening the
  constellations,
The glitterers in the black, to keep off,

Keep their distance,
While it works this out.

The rat understands suddenly. It bows and is still,
With a little beseeching of blood on its nose-end.

II THE RAT'S VISION

The rat hears the wind saying something in the straw
And the night-fields that have come up to the fence, leaning
    their silence,
The widowed land
With its trees that know how to cry

The rat sees the farm bulk of beam and stone
Wobbling like reflection on water.
The wind is pushing from the gulf
Through the old barbed wire in through the trenched
    gateway, past the gates of the ear, deep into the
    worked design of days,

Breathes onto the solitary snow crystal

The rat screeches
And 'Do not go' cry the dandelions, from their heads of folly
And 'Do not go' cry the yard cinders, who have no future,
    only their infernal aftermath
And 'Do not go' cries the cracked trough by the gate, fatalist
    of starlight and zero

'Stay' says the arrangement of stars

Forcing the rat's head down into godhead.

III THE RAT'S FLIGHT

The heaven shudders, a flame unrolled like a whip,
And the stars jolt in their sockets.
And the sleep-souls of eggs
Wince under the shot of shadow –

> That was the Shadow of the Rat
> Crossing into power
> Never to be buried

The horned Shadow of the Rat
Casting here by the door
A bloody gift for the dogs

While it supplants Hell.

Skylarks

I

The lark begins to go up
Like a warning
As if the globe were uneasy –

Barrel-chested for heights,
Like an Indian of the high Andes,

A whippet head, barbed like a hunting arrow,

But leaden
With muscle
For the struggle
Against
Earth's centre.

And leaden
For ballast
In the rocketing storms of the breath.

Leaden
Like a bullet
To supplant
Life from its centre.

II

Crueller than owl or eagle

A towered bird, shot through the crested head
With the command, Not die

But climb

Climb

Sing

Obedient as to death a dead thing.

III

I suppose you just gape and let your gaspings
Rip in and out through your voicebox
                              O lark

And sing inwards as well as outwards
Like a breaker of ocean milling the shingle
                                        O lark

O song, incomprehensibly both ways –
Joy! Help! Joy! Help!
                  O lark

IV

You stop to rest, far up, you teeter
Over the drop

But not stopping singing

Resting only for a second

Dropping just a little

Then up and up and up

Like a mouse with drowning fur
Bobbing and bobbing at the well-wall

Lamenting, mounting a little –

But the sun will not take notice
And the earth's centre smiles.

[35]

V

My idleness curdles
Seeing the lark labour near its cloud
Scrambling
In a nightmare difficulty
Up through the nothing

Its feathers thrash, its heart must be drumming like a motor,
As if it were too late, too late

Dithering in ether
Its song whirls faster and faster
And the sun whirls
The lark is evaporating
Till my eye's gossamer snaps
                    and my hearing floats back widely to earth

After which the sky lies blank open
Without wings, and the earth is a folded clod.

Only the sun goes silently and endlessly on with the lark's song.

VI

All the dreary Sunday morning
Heaven is a madhouse
With the voices and frenzies of the larks,

Squealing and gibbering and cursing

Heads flung back, as I see them,
Wings almost torn off backwards – far up

Like sacrifices set floating
The cruel earth's offerings

The mad earth's missionaries.

VII

Like those flailing flames
The lift from the fling of a bonfire
Claws dangling full of what they feed on

The larks carry their tongues to the last atom
Battering and battering their last sparks out at the limit –
So it's a relief, a cool breeze
When they've had enough, when they're burned out
And the sun's sucked them empty
And the earth gives them the O.K.

And they relax, drifting with changed notes

Dip and float, not quite sure if they may
Then they are sure and they stoop

And maybe the whole agony was for this

The plummeting dead drop

With long cutting screams buckling like razors

But just before they plunge into the earth

They flare and glide off low over grass, then up
To land on a wall-top, crest up,

Weightless,
Paid-up,
Alert,

Conscience perfect.

Manacled with blood,
Cuchulain listened bowed,
Strapped to his pillar (not to die prone)
Hearing the far crow
Guiding the near lark nearer
With its blind song

'*That some sorry little wight more feeble and misguided*
    than thyself
Take thy head
Thine ear
And thy life's career from thee.'

The Howling of Wolves

Is without world.

What are they dragging up and out on their long leashes
    of sound
That dissolve in the mid-air silence?

Then crying of a baby, in this forest of starving silences,
Brings the wolves running.
Tuning of a viola, in this forest delicate as an owl's ear,
Brings the wolves running – brings the steel traps clashing
    and slavering,
The steel furred to keep it from cracking in the cold,
The eyes that never learn how it has come about
That they must live like this,

That they must live

Innocence crept into minerals.

The wind sweeps through and the hunched wolf shivers.
It howls you cannot say whether out of agony or joy.

The earth is under its tongue,
A dead weight of darkness, trying to see through its eyes.
The wolf is living for the earth.
But the wolf is small, it comprehends little.

It goes to and fro, trailing its haunches and whimpering
    horribly.

It must feed its fur.

The night snows stars and the earth creaks.

Gnat-Psalm

When the gnats dance at evening
Scribbling on the air, sparring sparely,
Scrambling their crazy lexicon,
Shuffling their dumb Cabala,
Under leaf shadow

Leaves only leaves
Between them and the broad swipes of the sun
Leaves muffling the dusty stabs of the late sun
From their frail eyes and crepuscular temperaments

Dancing
Dancing
Writing on the air, rubbing out everything they write
Jerking their letters into knots, into tangles
Everybody everybody else's yoyo

Immense magnets fighting around a centre

Not writing and not fighting but singing
That the cycles of this Universe are no matter
That they are not afraid of the sun
That the one sun is too near
It blasts their song, which is of all the suns
That they are their own sun
Their own brimming over
At large in the nothing
Their wings blurring the blaze
Singing

That they are the nails
In the dancing hands and feet of the gnat-god
That they hear the wind suffering

Through the grass
And the evening tree suffering

The wind bowing with long cat-gut cries
And the long roads of dust
Dancing in the wind
The wind's dance, the death-dance, entering the mountain
And the cow dung villages huddling to dust

But not the gnats, their agility
Has outleaped that threshold
And hangs them a little above the claws of the grass
Dancing
Dancing
In the glove shadows of the sycamore

A dance never to be altered
A dance giving their bodies to be burned

And their mummy faces will never be used

Their little bearded faces
Weaving and bobbing on the nothing
Shaken in the air, shaken, shaken
And their feet dangling like the feet of victims

O little Hasids
Ridden to death by your own bodies
Riding your bodies to death
You are the angels of the only heaven!

And God is an Almighty Gnat!
You are the greatest of all the galaxies!
My hands fly in the air, they are follies
My tongue hangs up in the leaves
My thoughts have crept into crannies

Your dancing

Your dancing

Rolls my staring skull slowly away into outer space.

Wodwo

What am I? Nosing here, turning leaves over
Following a faint stain on the air to the river's edge
I enter water. What am I to split
The glassy grain of water looking upward I see the bed
Of the river above me upside down very clear
What am I doing here in mid-air? Why do I find
this frog so interesting as I inspect its most secret
interior and make it my own? Do these weeds
know me and name me to each other have they
seen me before, do I fit in their world? I seem
separate from the ground and not rooted but dropped
out of nothing casually I've no threads
fastening me to anything I can go anywhere
I seem to have been given the freedom
of this place what am I then? And picking
bits of bark off this rotten stump gives me
no pleasure and it's no use so why do I do it
me and doing that have coincided very queerly
But what shall I be called am I the first
have I an owner what shape am I what
shape am I am I huge if I go
to the end on this way past these trees and past these trees
till I get tired that's touching one wall of me
for the moment if I sit still how everything
stops to watch me I suppose I am the exact centre
but there's all this what is it roots
roots roots roots and here's the water
again very queer but I'll go on looking

That Moment

When the pistol muzzle oozing blue vapour
Was lifted away
Like a cigarette lifted from an ashtray

And the only face left in the world
Lay broken
Between hands that relaxed, being too late

And the trees closed forever
And the streets closed forever

And the body lay on the gravel
Of the abandoned world
Among abandoned utilities
Exposed to infinity forever

Crow had to start searching for something to eat.

Crow and the Birds

When the eagle soared clear through a dawn distilling of emerald
When the curlew trawled in seadusk through a chime of
    wineglasses
When the swallow swooped through a woman's song in a cavern
And the swift flicked through the breath of a violet

When the owl sailed clear of tomorrow's conscience
And the sparrow preened himself of yesterday's promise
And the heron laboured clear of the Bessemer upglare
And the bluetit zipped clear of lace panties
And the woodpecker drummed clear of the rotovator and the
    rose-farm
And the peewit tumbled clear of the laundromat

While the bullfinch plumped in the apple bud
And the goldfinch bulbed in the sun
And the wryneck crooked in the moon
And the dipper peered from the dewball

Crow spraddled head-down in the beach-garbage, guzzling a
    dropped ice-cream.

Crow Tyrannosaurus

Creation quaked voices –
It was a cortege
Of mourning and lament
Crow could hear and he looked around fearfully.

The swift's body fled past
Pulsating
With insects
And their anguish, all it had eaten.

The cat's body writhed
Gagging
A tunnel
Of incoming death-struggles, sorrow on sorrow.

And the dog was a bulging filterbag
Of all the deaths it had gulped for the flesh and the bones.
It could not digest their screeching finales.
Its shapeless cry was a blort of all those voices.

Even man he was a walking
Abattoir
Of innocents –
His brain incinerating their outcry.

Crow thought 'Alas
Alas ought I
To stop eating
And try to become the light?'

But his eye saw a grub. And his head, trapsprung, stabbed.
And he listened
And he heard
Weeping

Grubs   grubs   He stabbed   he stabbed
Weeping
Weeping

Weeping he walked and stabbed

Thus came the eye's
                    roundness
                              the ear's
                                    deafness.

Two Legends

I

Black was the without eye
Black the within tongue
Black was the heart
Black the liver, black the lungs
Unable to suck in light
Black the blood in its loud tunnel
Black the bowels packed in furnace
Black too the muscles
Striving to pull out into the light
Black the nerves, black the brain
With its tombed visions
Black also the soul, the huge stammer
Of the cry that, swelling, could not
Pronounce its sun.

II

Black is the wet otter's head, lifted.
Black is the rock, plunging in foam.
Black is the gall lying on the bed of the blood.

Black is the earth-globe, one inch under,
An egg of blackness
Where sun and moon alternate their weathers

To hatch a crow, a black rainbow
Bent in emptiness
                        over emptiness

But flying

Lineage

In the beginning was Scream
Who begat Blood
Who begat Eye
Who begat Fear
Who begat Wing
Who begat Bone
Who begat Granite
Who begat Violet
Who begat Guitar
Who begat Sweat
Who begat Adam
Who begat Mary
Who begat God
Who begat Nothing
Who begat Never
Never Never Never

Who begat Crow

Screaming for Blood
Grubs, crusts
Anything

Trembling featherless elbows in the nest's filth

Examination at the Womb-Door

Who owns these scrawny little feet?   *Death.*
Who owns this bristly scorched-looking face?   *Death.*
Who owns these still-working lungs?   *Death.*
Who owns this utility coat of muscles?   *Death.*
Who owns these unspeakable guts?   *Death.*
Who owns these questionable brains?   *Death.*
All this messy blood?   *Death.*
These minimum-efficiency eyes?   *Death.*
This wicked little tongue?   *Death.*
This occasional wakefulness?   *Death.*

Given, stolen, or held pending trial?
Held.

Who owns the whole rainy, stony earth?   *Death.*
Who owns all of space?   *Death.*

Who is stronger than hope?   *Death.*
Who is stronger than the will?   *Death.*
Stronger than love?   *Death.*
Stronger than life?   *Death.*

But who is stronger than death?
                              Me, evidently.

Pass, Crow.

Crow's Fall

When Crow was white he decided the sun was too white.
He decided it glared much too whitely.
He decided to attack it and defeat it.

He got his strength flush and in full glitter.
He clawed and fluffed his rage up.
He aimed his beak direct at the sun's centre.

He laughed himself to the centre of himself

And attacked.

At his battle cry trees grew suddenly old,
Shadows flattened.

But the sun brightened –
It brightened, and Crow returned charred black.

He opened his mouth but what came out was charred black.

'Up there,' he managed,
'Where white is black and black is white, I won.'

Owl's Song

He sang
How the swan blanched forever
How the wolf threw away its telltale heart
And the stars dropped their pretence
The air gave up appearances
Water went deliberately numb
The rock surrendered its last hope
And cold died beyond knowledge

He sang
How everything had nothing more to lose

Then sat still with fear

Seeing the clawtrack of star
Hearing the wingbeat of rock

And his own singing

Crow's Elephant Totem Song

Once upon a time
God made this Elephant.
Then it was delicate and small
It was not freakish at all
Or melancholy

The Hyenas sang in the scrub: You are beautiful –
They showed their scorched heads and grinning expressions
Like the half-rotted stumps of amputations –
We envy your grace
Waltzing through the thorny growth
O take us with you to the Land of Peaceful
O ageless eyes of innocence and kindliness
Lift us from the furnaces
And furies of our blackened faces
Within these hells we writhe
Shut in behind the bars of our teeth
In hourly battle with a death
The size of the earth
Having the strength of the earth.

So the Hyenas ran under the Elephant's tail
As like a lithe and rubber oval
He strolled gladly around inside his ease
But he was not God no it was not his
To correct the damned
In rage in madness then they lit their mouths
They tore out his entrails
They divided him among their several hells
To cry all his separate pieces
Swallowed and inflamed
Amidst paradings of infernal laughter.

At the Resurrection
The Elephant got himself together with correction
Deadfall feet and toothproof body and bulldozing bones
And completely altered brains
Behind aged eyes, that were wicked and wise.

So through the orange blaze and blue shadow
Of the afterlife, effortless and immense,
The Elephant goes his own way, a walking sixth sense,
And opposite and parallel
The sleepless Hyenas go
Along a leafless skyline trembling like an oven roof
With a whipped run
Their shame-flags tucked hard down
Over the gutsacks
Crammed with putrefying laughter
Blotched black with the leakage and seepings
And they sing: 'Ours is the land
Of loveliness and beautiful
Is the putrid mouth of the leopard
And the graves of fever
Because it is all we have –'
And they vomit their laughter.

And the Elephant sings deep in the forest-maze
About a star of deathless and painless peace
But no astronomer can find where it is.

Littleblood

O littleblood, hiding from the mountains in the mountains
Wounded by stars and leaking shadow
Eating the medical earth.

O littleblood, little boneless little skinless
Ploughing with a linnet's carcase
Reaping the wind and threshing the stones.

O littleblood, drumming in a cow's skull
Dancing with a gnat's feet
With an elephant's nose with a crocodile's tail.

Grown so wise grown so terrible
Sucking death's mouldy tits.

Sit on my finger, sing in my ear, O littleblood.

from Prometheus On His Crag

Prometheus On His Crag

Pestered by birds roosting and defecating,
· The chattering static of the wind-honed summit,
The clusterers to heaven, the sun-darkeners –

Shouted a world's end shout.
Then the swallow folded its barbs and fell,
The dove's bubble of fluorescence burst,

Nightingale and cuckoo
Plunged into padded forests where the woodpecker
Eyes bleached insane

Howled laughter into dead holes.
The birds became what birds have ever since been,
Scratching, probing, peering for a lost world –

A world of holy, happy notions shattered
By the shout
That brought Prometheus peace

And woke the vulture.

Prometheus On His Crag

Began to admire the vulture
It knew what it was doing

It went on doing it
Swallowing not only his liver
But managing also to digest its guilt

And hang itself again just under the sun
Like a heavenly weighing scales
Balancing the gift of life

And the cost of the gift
Without a tremor
As if both were nothing.

The Lamentable History of the Human Calf

O there was a maiden, a maiden, a maiden
And she was a knock-out.
Will you be my bride, I sighed, I cried, I was ready to die.
And she replied, what did she reply?

'Give me your nose, for a kiss' she sighed. 'It's a fair pawn!'
  So I sliced off my nose
And she fed it to her puppy.

Lady, are you satisfied?

'O give me your ears, to share my fears, in the night, in my bed,
    where nobody hears, my darling!'
So I sliced off my ears
And she fed them to her puppy.

'Now let me have your legs, lest they carry you far,
  O my darling, far from my side,' she cried.
So I chopped off my legs and she gave them to her puppy.

Lady, are you happy?

'O I want your heart, your heart, your heart, will it never be
    mine? Let me hold it,' she cried.
So I sliced me wide, and I ripped out the part
And she fed it to her puppy.

Lady, are you satisfied?

'O give me your liver, or I'll leave you forever.
Give me your tongue, your tongue, your tongue
Lest it whisper to another.
Give me your lungs that hurt you with their sighs,'
She cried.

With tears of love, with tears of love, I hacked out those dainties
And she fed them to her puppy.

Lady, are you satisfied?

'O give me your eyes, your rolling eyes,
That splash me with their tears, that go roving after others.
And give me your brains, that give you such pains
With doubting of my love, with doubting of my love.
And give me your arms, that all night long when you're far from
    my side they'll clasp me, clasp me'
And she cried, 'I'll be your bride!'
So I tore out my eyes and I gouged out my brains and I sawed
    off my arms and I gave them to my darling
And she fed them to her puppy.

Lady, are you satisfied?

'No, give me your skin, that holds you in,
O pour out your blood in a bowl and let me drink it, be mine.
O slice off your flesh and I'll nibble your bones, my darling!'
So I dragged off my skin and I brimmed it with my blood and I
    rolled up my flesh and I basketted my bones and I laid them
    at her door and she cried and she cried

Puppy, puppy, puppy.

Lady, I said, though I'm nothing but a soul, I have paid down
    the price, now come to be my bride.
But the puppy had grown, the puppy was a dog, was a big fat
    bitch, and my darling wept

'Take my dog,' she wept, 'O take it.
You are only a soul, how can we now be married?
So take my dog for this dog it is my soul,
I give you my soul!' And she gave me her dog.

Lady are you satisfied?

Now I live with a bitch an old sour bitch now I live with a
bitch a bitch a bitch so I live with a bitch an old sour
bitch and there was a maiden a maiden a maiden . . .

Swifts

Fifteenth of May. Cherry blossom. The swifts
Materialise at the tip of a long scream
Of needle. 'Look! They're back! Look!' And they're gone
On a steep

Controlled scream of skid
Round the house-end and away under the cherries. Gone.
Suddenly flickering in sky summit, three or four together,
Gnat-whisp frail, and hover-searching, and listening

For air-chills – are they too early? With a bowing
Power-thrust to left, then to right, then a flicker they
Tilt into a slide, a tremble for balance,
Then a lashing down disappearance

Behind elms.
                        They've made it again,
Which means the globe's still working, the Creation's
Still waking refreshed, our summer's
Still all to come –
                        And here they are, here they are again
Erupting across yard stones
Shrapnel-scatter terror. Frog-gapers,
Speedway goggles, international mobsters –

A bolas of three or four wire screams
Jockeying across each other
On their switchback wheel of death.
They swat past, hard-fletched,

Veer on the hard air, toss up over the roof,
And are gone again. Their mole-dark labouring,
Their lunatic limber scramming frenzy
And their whirling blades

Sparkle out into blue –
                    Not ours any more.
Rats ransacked their nests so now they shun us.
Round luckier houses now
They crowd their evening dirt-track meetings,

Racing their discords, screaming as if speed-burned,
Head-height, clipping the doorway
With their leaden velocity and their butterfly lightness,
Their too much power, their arrow-thwack into the eaves.

Every year a first-fling, nearly-flying
Misfit flopped in our yard,
Groggily somersaulting to get airborne.
He bat-crawled on his tiny useless feet, tangling his flails

Like a broken toy, and shrieking thinly
Till I tossed him up – then suddenly he flowed away under
His bowed shoulders of enormous swimming power,
Slid away along levels wobbling

On the fine wire they have reduced life to,
And crashed among the raspberries.
Then followed fiery hospital hours
In a kitchen. The moustached goblin savage

Nested in a scarf. The bright blank
Blind, like an angel, to my meat-crumbs and flies.
Then eyelids resting. Wasted clingers curled.
The inevitable balsa death.

                    Finally burial
For the husk
Of my little Apollo –

The charred scream
Folded in its huge power.

Mackerel Song

While others sing the mackerel's armour
His stub scissor head and his big blurred eye
And the flimsy savagery of his onset
I sing his simple hunger.

While others sing the mackerel's swagger
His miniature ocelot oil-green stripings
And his torpedo solidity of thump
I sing his gormless plenty.

While others sing the mackerel's fury
The belly-tug lightning-trickle of his evasions
And the wrist-thick muscle of his last word
I sing his loyal come-back.

While others sing the mackerel's acquaintance
The soap of phosphorus he lathers on your fingers
The midget gut and the tropical racer's torso
I sing his scorched sweetness.

While others sing the mackerel's demise
His ultimatum to be cooked instantly
And the shock of his decay announcement
I sing how he makes the rich summer seas

A million times richer

With the gift of his millions.

Work and Play

The swallow of summer, she toils all summer,
A blue-dark knot of glittering voltage,
A whiplash swimmer, a fish of the air.
    But the serpent of cars that crawls through the dust
    In shimmering exhaust
    Searching to slake
    Its fever in ocean
    Will play and be idle or else it will bust.

The swallow of summer, the barbed harpoon,
She flings from the furnace, a rainbow of purples,
Dips her glow in the pond and is perfect.
    But the serpent of cars that collapsed at the beach
    Disgorges its organs
    A scamper of colours
    Which roll like tomatoes
    Nude as tomatoes
    With sand in their creases
    To cringe in the sparkle of rollers and screech.

The swallow of summer, the seamstress of summer,
She scissors the blue into shapes and she sews it,
She draws a long thread and she knots it at corners.
    But the holiday people
    Are laid out like wounded
    Flat as in ovens
    Roasting and basting
    With faces of torment as space burns them blue
    Their heads are transistors
    Their teeth grit on sand grains
    Their lost kids are squalling

While man-eating flies
Jab electric shock needles but what can they do?

They can climb in their cars with raw bodies, raw faces
And start up the serpent
And headache it homeward
A car full of squabbles
And sobbing and stickiness
With sand in their crannies
Inhaling petroleum
That pours from the foxgloves
While the evening swallow
The swallow of summer, cartwheeling through crimson,
Touches the honey-slow river and turning
Returns to the hand stretched from under the eaves –
A boomerang of rejoicing shadow.

A Cranefly in September

She is struggling through grass-mesh – not flying,
Her wide-winged, stiff, weightless basket-work of limbs
Rocking, like an antique wain, a top-heavy ceremonial cart
Across mountain summits
(Not planing over water, dipping her tail)
But blundering with long strides, long reachings, reelings
And ginger-glistening wings
From collision to collision.
Aimless in no particular direction,
Just exerting her last to escape out of the overwhelming
Of whatever it is, legs, grass,
The garden, the county, the country, the world –

Sometimes she rests long minutes in the grass forest
Like a fairytale hero, only a marvel can help her.
She cannot fathom the mystery of this forest
In which, for instance, this giant watches –
The giant who knows she cannot be helped in any way.

Her jointed bamboo fuselage,
Her lobster shoulders, and her face
Like a pinhead dragon, with its tender moustache,
And the simple colourless church windows of her wings
Will come to an end, in mid-search, quite soon.
Everything about her, every perfected vestment
Is already superfluous.
The monstrous excess of her legs and curly feet
Are a problem beyond her.
The calculus of glucose and chitin inadequate
To plot her through the infinities of the stems.

The frayed apple leaves, the grunting raven, the defunct tractor
Sunk in nettles, wait with their multiplications
Like other galaxies.
The sky's Northward September procession, the vast soft
    armistice,
Like an Empire on the move,
Abandons her, tinily embattled
With her cumbering limbs and cumbered brain.

The Stag

While the rain fell on the November woodland shoulder of
   Exmoor
While the traffic jam along the road honked and shouted
Because the farmers were parking wherever they could
And scrambling to the bank-top to stare through the tree-fringe
Which was leafless,
The stag ran through his private forest.

While the rain drummed on the roofs of the parked cars
And the kids inside cried and daubed their chocolate and fought
And mothers and aunts and grandmothers
Were a tangle of undoing sandwiches and screwed-round
   gossiping heads
Steaming up the windows,
The stag loped through his favourite valley.

While the blue horsemen down in the boggy meadow
Sodden nearly black, on sodden horses,
Spaced as at a military parade,
Moved a few paces to the right and a few to the left and felt
   rather foolish
Looking at the brown impassable river,
The stag came over the last hill of Exmoor.

While everybody high-kneed it to the bank-top all along the road
Where steady men in oilskins were stationed at binoculars,
And the horsemen by the river galloped anxiously this way
   and that
And the cry of hounds came tumbling invisibly with their echoes
   down through the draggle of trees,
Swinging across the wall of dark woodland,
The stag dropped into a strange country.

And turned at the river
Hearing the hound-pack smash the undergrowth, hearing the
    bell-note
Of the voice that carried all the others,
Then while his limbs all cried different directions to his lungs,
    which only wanted to rest,
The blue horsemen on the bank opposite
Pulled aside the camouflage of their terrible planet.

And the stag doubled back weeping and looking for home up a
    valley and down a valley
While the strange trees struck at him and the brambles lashed him,
And the strange earth came galloping after him carrying the
    loll–tongued hounds to fling all over him
And his heart became just a club beating his ribs and his own
    hooves shouted with hounds' voices,
And the crowd on the road got back into their cars
Wet-through and disappointed.

from Gaudete

Calves harshly parted from their mamas
Stumble through all the hedges in the country
Hither thither crying day and night
Till their throats will only grunt and whistle.

After some days, a stupor sadness
Collects them again in their field.
They will never stray any more.
From now on, they only want each other.

So much for calves.
As for the tiger
He lies still
Like left luggage

He is roaming the earth light, unseen.

He is safe.

Heaven and hell have both adopted him.

A Solstice

Drip-tree stillness. Spring-feeling elation
Of mid-morning oxygen. There is a yeasty simmering
Over the land – all compass points are trembling,
Bristling with starlings, hordes out of Siberia,
Bubbly and hopeful.

We stand in the mist-rawness
Of the sodden earth. Four days to Christmas.
We can hear the grass seeping.
                              Now a wraith-smoke
Writhes up from a far field, condenses
On a frieze of goblin hedge-oaks, sizzling
Like power-pylons in mist.

We ease our way into this landscape.
Casual midnightish draughts, in the soaking stillness.
Itch of starlings is everywhere.
                              The gun
Is old, rust-ugly, single-barrelled, borrowed
For a taste of English sport. And you have come
From eighteen years Australian estrangement
And twelve thousand miles in thin air
To walk again on the small hills of the West,
In the ruby and emerald lights, the leaf-wet oils
Of your memory's masterpiece.
                              Hedge-sparrows
Needle the bramble-mass undergrowth
With their weepy warnings.
                              You have the gun.
We harden our eyes. We are alert.
The gun-muzzle is sniffing. And the broad land

Tautens into wilder, nervier contrasts
Of living and unliving. Our eyes feather over it
As over a touchy detonator.

Bootprints between the ranks of baby barley
Heel and toe we go
Narrowed behind the broad gaze of the gun
Down the long woodside. I am your dog.

Now I get into the wood. I push parallel
And slightly ahead of you – the idea
Is to flush something for the gun's amusement.
I go delicate. I don't want to panic
My listeners into a crouch–freeze.
I want them to keep their initiative
And slip away, confident, impudent,
Out across your front.
                              Pigeons, too far,
Burst up from under the touch
Of our furthest listenings. A bramble
Claws across my knee, and a blackbird
Five yards off explodes its booby-trap
Shattering wetly
Black and yellow alarm-dazzlings, and a long string
Of fireworks down the wood. It settles
To a hacking chatter and that blade-ringing –
Like a flint on an axe-head.
                              I wait.
That startled me too.
I know I am a Gulliver now
Tied by my every slightest move
To a thousand fears. But I move –
And a jay, invisibly somewhere safe,
Starts pretending to tear itself in half

From the mouth backward. With three screams
It scares itself to silence.
                            The whole wood
Has hidden in the wood. Its mossy tunnels
Seem to age as we listen. A raven
Dabs a single charcoal toad-croak
Into the finished picture.

                            I come out
To join you in the field. We need a new plan
To surprise something.
                            But as I come over the wire
You are pointing, silent.
I look. One hundred yards
Down the woodside, somebody
Is watching us.

A strangely dark fox
Motionless in his robe of office
Is watching us. It is a shock.

Too deep in the magic wood, suddenly
We meet the magician.
                            Then he's away –
A slender figurine, dark and witchy,
A rocking nose-down lollop, and the load of tail
Floating behind him, over the swell of faint corn
Into the long arm of woodland opposite.

The gun does nothing. But we gaze after
Like men who have been given a secret sign.
We are studying the changed expression
Of that straggle of scrub and poor trees
Which is now the disguise of a fox.

[73]

And the gun is thinking. The gun
Is working its hunter's magic.
It is transforming us, there in the dull mist,
To two suits of cold armour –
Empty of all but a strange new humming,
A mosquito of primaeval excitements.

And as we start to walk out over the field
The gun smiles.

The fox will be under brambles.
He has set up all his antennae,
His dials are glowing and quivering,
Every hair adjusts itself
To our coming.

                              Will he wait in the copse
Till we've made our move, as if this were a game
He is interested to play?
Or has he gone through and away over further fields,
Or down and into the blueish mass and secrecy
Of the main wood?

Under a fat oak, where the sparse copse
Joins the main wood, you lean in ambush.

Well out in the field, talking to air
Like quiet cogs, I stroll to the top of the strip –
Then pierce it, clumsy as a bullock, a careless trampling
Like purposeless machinery, towards you,
Noisy enough for you to know
Where not to point your blind gun.

Somewhere between us
The fox is inspecting me, magnified.
And now I tangle all his fears with a silence,

Then a sudden abrupt advance, then again silence,
Then a random change of direction –

And almost immediately –
Almost before I've decided we are serious –
The blast wall hits me, the gun bang bursts
Like a paper bag in my face,
The whole day bursts like a paper bag –

But a new world is created instantly
With no visible change.

I pause. I call. You do not answer.
Everything is just as it had been.
The corroded blackberry leaves,
The crooked naked trees, fingering sky
Are all the usual careful shapes
Of the usual silence.

I go forward. And now I see you,
As if you had missed,
Leaning against your tree, casual.

But between us, on the tussocky ground,
Somebody is struggling with something.

An elegant gentleman, beautifully dressed,
Is struggling there, tangled with something,
And biting at something
With his flashing mouth. It is himself
He is tangled with. I come close
As if I might be of help.
But there is no way out.
It is himself he is biting,
Bending his head far back, and trying
To bite his shoulder. He has no time for me.

Blood beneath him is spoiling
The magnificent sooted russet
Of his overcoat, and the flawless laundering
Of his shirt. He is desperate
To get himself up on his feet,
And if he could catch the broken pain
In his teeth, and pull it out of his shoulder,
He still has some hope, because
The long brown grass is the same
As it was before, and the trees
Have not changed in any way,
And the sky continues the same –

It is doing the impossible deliberately
To set the gun-muzzle at his chest
And funnel that sky-bursting bang
Through a sudden blue pit in his fur
Into the earth beneath him.

He cannot believe it has happened.

His chin sinks forward, and he half-closes his mouth
In a smile
Of ultimate bitterness,
And half closes his eyes
In a fineness beyond pain –

And it is a dead fox in the dank woodland.
And you stand over him
Meeting your first real Ancient Briton
In eighteen years.
And I stand awake – as one wakes
From what feels like a cracking blow on the head.

That second shot has ruined his skin.

We chop his tail off
Thick and long as a forearm, and black.
Then bundle him and his velvet legs
His bag of useless jewels,
The phenomenal technology inside his head,
Into a hole, under a bulldozed stump,
Like picnic rubbish. There the memory ends.

We must have walked away.

from Orts

The white shark
With its strength of madness

The mutt-faced hyena
Trailing its half-dance

The rat
With its file

The gull, vomiting its laughter
And gulping it in again
Like intestines hanging from the mouth

– the thorn
With its petals.

Only a Little Sleep, a Little Slumber

And suddenly you
Have not a word to say for yourself.

Only a little knife, a small incision,
A snickety nick in the brain
And you drop off, like a polyp.

Only a crumb of fungus,
A pulp of mouldy tinder
And you flare, fluttering, black out like a firework.

Who are you, in the nest among the bones?
You are the shyest bird among birds.

'I am the last of my kind.'

The Owl Flower

Big terror descends.

A drumming glare, a flickering face of flames.

Something writhes apart into a signal,
Fiendish, a filament of incandescence.

As it were a hair.

In the maelstrom's eye,
In the core of the brimming heaven-blossom,
Under the tightening whorl of plumes, a mote
Scalds in dews.

A leaf of the earth
Applies to it, a cooling health.

A coffin spins in the torque.
Wounds flush with sap, headful of pollen,
Wet with nectar
The dead one stirs.

A mummy grain is cracking its grimace
In the cauldron of tongues.

The ship of flowers
Nudges the wharf of skin.

The egg-stone
Bursts among broody petals –

And a staggering thing
Fired with rainbows, raw with cringing heat,

Blinks at the source.

The Risen

He stands, filling the doorway
In the shell of earth.

He lifts wings, he leaves the remains of something,
A mess of offal, muddled as an afterbirth.

His each wingbeat – a convict's release.
What he carries will be plenty.

He slips behind the world's brow
As music escapes its skull, its clock and its skyline.

Under his sudden shadow, flames cry out among thickets.
When he soars, his shape

Is a cross, eaten by light,
On the Creator's face.

He shifts world weirdly as sunspots
Emerge as earthquakes.

A burning unconsumed,
A whirling tree –

Where he alights
A skin sloughs from a leafless apocalypse.

On his lens
Each atom engraves with a diamond.

In the wind-fondled crucible of his splendour
The dirt becomes God.

But when will he land
On a man's wrist.

And the Falcon came

The gunmetal feathers
Of would not be put aside, would not falter.

The wing-knuckles
Of dividing the mountain, of hurling the world away
     behind him.

With the bullet-brow
Of burying himself head-first and ahead
Of his delicate bones, into the target
Collision.

The talons
Of a first, last, single blow
Of grasping complete the crux of rays.

With the tooled bill
Of plucking out the ghost
And feeding it to his eye-flame

Of stripping down the loose, hot flutter of earth
To its component parts
For the reconstitution of Falcon.

With the eye
Of explosion of Falcon.

The Skylark came

With its effort hooked to the sun, a swinging ladder

With its song
A labour of its whole body
Thatching the sun with bird-joy

To keep off the rains of weariness
The snows of extinction

With its labour
Of a useless excess, lifting what can only fall

With its crest
Which it intends to put on the sun

Which it meanwhile wears itself
So earth can be crested

With its song
Erected between dark and dark

The lark that lives and dies
In the service of its crest.

The Wild Duck

                                    got up with a cry
Shook off her Arctic swaddling

Pitched from the tower of the North Wind
And came spanking across water

The wild duck, fracturing egg-zero,
Left her mother the snow in her shawl of stars
Abandoned her father the black wind in his beard of stars

Got up out of the ooze before dawn

Now hangs her whispering arrival
Between earth-glitter and heaven-glitter

Calling softly to the fixed lakes

As earth gets up in the frosty dark, at the back of the Pole Star
And flies into dew
Through the precarious crack of light

Quacking Wake Wake

The Swift comes the swift

Casts aside the two-arm two-leg article –
The pain instrument
Flesh and soft entrails and nerves, and is off.

Hurls itself as if again beyond where it fell among roofs
Out through the lightning-split in the great oak of light

One wing below mineral limit
One wing above dream and number

Shears between life and death

Whiskery snarl-gape already gone ahead
The eyes in possession ahead

Screams guess its trajectory
Meteorite puncturing the veils of worlds

Whipcrack, the ear's glimpse
Is the smudge it leaves

Hunting the winged mote of death into the sun's retina
Picking the nymph of life
Off the mirror of the lake of atoms

Till the Swift
Who falls out of the blindness, swims up
From the molten, rejoins itself

Shadow to shadow – resumes proof, nests
Papery ashes
Of the uncontainable burning.

The Unknown Wren

Hidden in Wren, sings only Wren. He sings
World-proof Wren
In thunderlight, at wrestling daybreak. Wren unalterable
In the wind-buffed wood.

Wren is here, but nearly out of control –
A blur of throbbings –
Electrocution by the god of wrens –
A battle-frenzy, a transfiguration –

Wren is singing in the wet bush.
His song sings him, every feather is a tongue
He is a song-ball of tongues –
The head squatted back, the pin-beak stretching to
     swallow the sky

And the wings quiver-lifting, as in death-rapture
Every feather a wing beating,
Wren is singing Wren – Wren of Wrens!
While his feet knot to a twig.

Imminent death only makes the wren more Wren-like
As harder sunlight, and realler earth-light.
Wren reigns! Wren is in power!
Under his upstart tail.

And when Wren sleeps even the star-drape heavens are
     a dream
Earth is just a bowl of ideas.

But now the lifted sun and the drenched woods rejoice
     with trembling –

WREN OF WRENS!

And Owl

Floats, a masked soul listening for death.
Death listening for a soul.
Small mouths and their incriminations are suspended.
Only the centre moves.

Constellations stand in awe. And the trees very still, the fields
    very still
As the Owl becalms deeper
To stillness.
Two eyes, fixed in the heart of heaven.

Nothing is neglected, in the Owl's stare.
The womb opens and the cry comes
And the shadow of the creature
Circumscribes its fate. And the Owl

Screams, again ripping the bandages off
Because of the shape of its throat, as if it were a torture
Because of the shape of its face, as if it were a prison
Because of the shape of its talons, as if they were inescapable.

Heaven screams. Earth screams. Heaven eats. Earth is eaten.

And earth eats and heaven is eaten.

The Dove Came

Her breast big with rainbows
She was knocked down

The dove came, her wings clapped lightning
That scattered like twigs
She was knocked down

The dove came, her voice of thunder
A piling heaven of silver and violet
She was knocked down

She gave the flesh of her breast, and they ate her
She gave the milk of her blood, they drank her

The dove came again, a sun-blinding

And ear could no longer hear

Mouth was a disembowelled bird
Where the tongue tried to stir like a heart

And the dove alit
In the body of thorns.

Now deep in the dense body of thorns
A soft thunder
Nests her rainbows.

The Crow came to Adam

And lifted his eyelid
And whispered in his ear

Who has heard the Crow's love-whisper?
Or the Crow's news?

Adam woke.

And the Phoenix has come

Its voice
Is the blade of the desert, a fighting of light
Its voice dangles glittering
In the soft valley of dew

Its voice flies flaming and dripping flame
Slowly across the dusty sky
Its voice burns in a rich heap
Of mountains that seem to melt

Its feathers shake from the eye
Its ashes smoke from the breath

Flesh trembles
The altar of its death and its birth

Where it descends
Where it offers itself up

And naked the newborn
Laughs in the blaze

Curlews

I

They lift
Out of the maternal watery blue lines

Stripped of all but their cry
Some twists of near-inedible sinew

They slough off
The robes of bilberry blue
The cloud-stained bogland

They veer up and eddy away over
The stone horns

They trail a long, dangling, falling aim
Across water

Lancing their voices
Through the skin of this light

Drinking the nameless and naked
Through trembling bills.

II

Curlews in April
Hang their harps over the misty valleys

A wobbling water-call
A wet-footed god of the horizons

New moons sink into the heather
And full golden moons

Bulge over spent walls.

The Weasels We Smoked out of the Bank

Ran along the rowan branch, a whole family,
Furious with ill-contained lightning
Over the ferny falls of clattering coolant.

After the time-long Creation
Of this hill-sculpture, this prone, horizon-long
Limb-jumble of near-female

The wild gentle god of everywhereness
Worships her, in a lark-rapture silence.

But the demons who did all the labouring
Run in and out of her holes

Crackling with redundant energy.

The Canal's Drowning Black

Bred wild leopards – among the pale depth fungus.
Loach. Torpid, ginger-bearded, secret
Prehistory of the canal's masonry,
With little cupid mouths.

Five inches huge!
On the slime-brink, over bridge reflections,
I teetered. Then a ringing, skull-jolt stamp
And their beards flowered sudden anemones

All down the sunken cliff. A mad-house thrill –
The stonework's tiny eyes, two feet, three feet,
Four feet down through my reflection
Watched for my next move.

Their schooldays were over.
Peeping man was no part of their knowledge.
So when a monkey god, a Martian
Tickled their underchins with his net rim

They snaked out and over the net rim easy
Back into the oligocene –
Only restrained by a mesh of kitchen curtain.
Then flopped out of their ocean-shifting aeons

Into a two pound jam-jar
On a windowsill
Blackened with acid rain fall-out
From Manchester's rotten lung.

Next morning, Mount Zion's
Cowled, Satanic majesty behind me

I lobbed – one by one – high through the air
The stiff, pouting, failed, paled new moons

Back into their Paradise and mine.

The Long Tunnel Ceiling

Of the main road canal bridge
Cradled black stalactite reflections.
That was the place for dark loach!

At the far end, the Moderna blanket factory
And the bushy mask of Hathershelf above it
Peered in through the cell-window.

Lorries from Bradford, baled with plump and towering
Wools and cotton met, above my head,
Lorries from Rochdale, and ground past each other
Making that cavern of air and water tremble –

Suddenly a crash!
The long gleam-ponderous watery echo shattered.

And at last it had begun!
That could only have been a brick from the ceiling!
The bridge was starting to collapse!

But the canal swallowed its scare,
The heavy mirror reglassed itself,
And the black arch gazed up at the black arch.

Till a brick
Rose through its eruption – hung massive
Then slammed back with a shock and a shattering.

An ingot!
Holy of holies! A treasure!
A trout
Nearly as long as my arm, solid
Molten pig of many a bronze loach!

There he lay – lazy – a free lord,
Ignoring me. Caressing, dismissing
The eastward easing traffic of drift,
Master of the Pennine Pass!

Found in some thin glitter among mean sandstone,
High under ferns, high up near sour heather,

Brought down on a midnight cloudburst
In a shake-up of heaven and the hills
When the streams burst with zig-zags and explosions

A seed
Of the wild god now flowering for me
Such a tigerish, dark, breathing lily
Between the tyres, under the tortured axles.

Cock-Crows

I stood on a dark summit, among dark summits –
Tidal dawn splitting heaven from earth,
The oyster
Opening to taste gold.

And I heard the cock-crows kindling in the valley
Under the mist –
They were sleepy,
Bubbling deep in the valley cauldron.

Then one or two tossed clear, like soft rockets
And sank back again dimming.

Then soaring harder, brighter, higher
Tearing the mist,
Bubble-glistenings flung up and bursting to light
Brightening the undercloud,
The fire-crests of the cocks – the sickle shouts,
Challenge against challenge, answer to answer,
Hooking higher,
Clambering up the sky as they melted,
Hanging smouldering from the night's fringes.

Till the whole valley brimmed with cock-crows,
A magical soft mixture boiling over,
Spilling and sparkling into other valleys

Lobbed-up horse-shoes of glow-swollen metal
From sheds in back-gardens, hen-cotes, farms
Sinking back mistily

Till the last spark died, and embers paled

And the sun climbed into its wet sack
For the day's work

While the dark rims hardened
Over the smoke of towns, from holes in earth.

Feeding out-wintering cattle at twilight

The wind is inside the hill.
The wood is a struggle – like a wood
Struggling through a wood. A panic
Only just holds off – every gust
Breaches the sky-walls and it seems, this time,
The whole sea of air will pour through,
The thunder will take deep hold, roots
Will have to come out, every loose thing
Will have to lift and go. And the cows, dark lumps of dusk
Stand waiting, like nails in a tin roof.
For the crucial moment, taking the strain
In their stirring stillness. As if their hooves
Held their field in place, held the hill
To its trembling shape. Night-thickness
Purples in the turmoil, making
Everything more alarming. Unidentifiable, tiny
Birds go past like elf-bolts.
Battling the hay-bales from me, the cows
Jostle and crush, like hulls blown from their moorings
And piling at the jetty. The wind
Has got inside their wintry buffalo skins,
Their wild woolly bulk-heads, their fierce, joyful breathings
And the reckless strength of their necks.
What do they care, their hooves
Are knee-deep in porridge of earth –
The hay blows luminous tatters from their chewings,
A fiery loss, frittering downwind,
Snatched away over the near edge
Where the world becomes water
Thundering like a flood-river at night.

They grunt happily, half-dissolved
On their steep, hurtling brink, as I flounder back
Towards headlights.

17 February 1974

Foxhunt

Two days after Xmas, near noon, as I listen
The hounds behind the hill
Are changing ground, a cloud of excitements,
Their voices like rusty, reluctant
Rolling stock being shunted. The hunt
Has tripped over a fox
At the threshold of the village. A crow in the fir
Is inspecting his nesting site, and he expostulates
At the indecent din. A blackbird
Starts up its cat-alarm. The grey-cloud mugginess
Of the year in its pit trying to muster
Enough energy to start opening again
Roars distantly. Everything sodden. The fox
Is flying, taking his first lesson
From the idiot pack-noise, the puppyish whine-yelps
Curling up like hounds' tails, and the gruff military barkers:
A machine with only two products:
Dog-shit and dead foxes. Lorry engines
As usual modulating on the main street hill
Complicate the air, and the fox runs in a suburb
Of indifferent civilized noises. Now the yelpings
Enrich their brocade, thickening closer
In the maze of wind-currents. The orchards
And the hedges stand in coma. The pastures
Have got off so far lightly, are firm, cattle
Still nose hopefully, as if spring might be here
Missing out winter. Big lambs
Are organizing their gangs in gateways. The fox
Hangs his silver tongue in the world of noise
Over his spattering paws. Will he run

Till his muscles suddenly turn to iron,
Till blood froths his mouth as his lungs tatter,
Till his feet are raw blood-sticks and his tail
Trails thin as a rat's? Or will he
Make a mistake, jump the wrong way, jump right
Into the hound's mouth? As I write this down
He runs still fresh, with all his chances before him.

27 December 1975

Roe-deer

In the dawn-dirty light, in the biggest snow of the year
Two blue-dark deer stood in the road, alerted.

They had happened into my dimension
The moment I was arriving just there.

They planted their two or three years of secret deerhood
Clear on my snow-screen vision of the abnormal

And hesitated in the all-way disintegration
And stared at me. And so for some lasting seconds

I could think the deer were waiting for me
To remember the password and sign

That the curtain had blown aside for a moment
And there where the trees were no longer trees, nor the road
    a road

The deer had come for me.

Then they ducked through the hedge, and upright they rode
    their legs
Away downhill over a snow-lonely field

Towards tree dark – finally
Seeming to eddy and glide and fly away up

Into the boil of big flakes.
The snow took them and soon their nearby hoofprints as well

Revising its dawn inspiration
Back to the ordinary.

13 February 1973

[103]

February 17th

A lamb could not get born. Ice wind
Out of a downpour dishclout sunrise. The mother
Lay on the mudded slope. Harried, she got up
And the blackish lump bobbed at her back-end
Under her tail. After some hard galloping,
Some manoeuvring, much flapping of the backward
Lump head of the lamb looking out,
I caught her with a rope. Laid her, head uphill
And examined the lamb. A blood-ball swollen
Tight in its black felt, its mouth gap
Squashed crooked, tongue stuck out, black-purple,
Strangled by its mother. I felt inside,
Past the noose of mother-flesh, into the slippery
Muscled tunnel, fingering for a hoof,
Right back to the port-hole of the pelvis.
But there was no hoof. He had stuck his head out too early
And his feet could not follow. He should have
Felt his way, tip-toe, his toes
Tucked up under his nose
For a safe landing. So I kneeled wrestling
With her groans. No hand could squeeze past
The lamb's neck into her interior
To hook a knee. I roped that baby head
And hauled till she cried out and tried
To get up and I saw it was useless. I went
Two miles for the injection and a razor.
Sliced the lamb's throat-strings, levered with a knife
Between the vertebrae and brought the head off
To stare at its mother, its pipes sitting in the mud
With all earth for a body. Then pushed

The neck-stump right back in, and as I pushed
She pushed. She pushed crying and I pushed gasping.
And the strength
Of the birth push and the push of my thumb
Against that wobbly vertebra were deadlock,
A to-fro futility. Till I forced
A hand past and got a knee. Then like
Pulling myself to the ceiling with one finger
Hooked in a loop, timing my effort
To her birth push groans, I pulled against
The corpse that would not come. Till it came.
And after it the long, sudden, yolk-yellow
Parcel of life
In a smoking slither of oils and soups and syrups –
And the body lay born, beside the hacked-off head.

17 February 1974

Coming down through Somerset

I flash-glimpsed in the headlights – the high moment
Of driving through England – a killed badger
Sprawled with helpless legs. Yet again
Manoeuvred lane-ends, retracked, waited
Out of decency for headlights to die,
Lifted by one warm hindleg in the world-night
A slain badger. August dust-heat. Beautiful,
Beautiful, warm, secret beast. Bedded him
Passenger, bleeding from the nose. Brought him close
Into my life. Now he lies on the beam
Torn from a great building. Beam waiting two years
To be built into new building. Summer coat
Not worth skinning off him. His skeleton – for the future.
Fangs, handsome concealed. Flies, drumming,
Bejewel his transit. Heatwave ushers him hourly
Towards his underworlds. A grim day of flies
And sunbathing. Get rid of that badger.
A night of shrunk rivers, glowing pastures,
Sea-trout shouldering up through trickles. Then the sun again
Waking like a torn-out eye. How strangely
He stays on into the dawn – how quiet
The dark bear-claws, the long frost-tipped guard hairs!
Get rid of that badger today.
And already the flies.
More passionate, bringing their friends. I don't want
To bury and waste him. Or skin him (it is too late).
Or hack off his head and boil it
To liberate his masterpiece skull. I want him
To stay as he is. Sooty gloss-throated,
With his perfect face. Paws so tired,

Power-body relegated. I want him
To stop time. His strength staying, bulky,
Blocking time. His rankness, his bristling wildness,
His thrillingly painted face.
A badger on my moment of life.
Not years ago, like the others, but now.
I stand
Watching his stillness, like an iron nail
Driven, flush to the head,
Into a yew post. Something has to stay.

8 August 1975

While she chews sideways

He gently noses the high point of her rear-end
Then lower and on each side of the tail,
Then flattens one ear, and gazes away, then decidedly turns,
    wheels,
And moves in on the pink-eyed long-horned grey.
He sniffs the length of her spine, arching slightly
And shitting a tumble-thud shit as he does so.
Now he's testy.
He takes a push at the crazy galloway with the laid back ears.
Now strolling away from them all, his aim at the corner gate.
He is scratching himself on the fence, his vibration
Travels the length of the wire.
His barrel bulk is a bit ugly.
As bulls go he's no beauty.
His balls swing in their sock, one side idle.
His skin is utility white, shit-patched,
Pink sinewed at the groin, and the dewlap nearly naked.
A feathery long permed bush of silky white tail –
It hangs straight like a bell rope
From the power-strake of his spine.
He eats steadily, not a cow in the field is open,
His gristly pinkish head, like a shaved blood-hound,
Jerking at the grass.
Overmuch muscle on the thighs, jerk-weight settling
Of each foot, as he eats forward.
His dangle tassel swings, his whole mind
Anchored to it and now dormant.
He's feeding disgustedly, impatiently, carelessly.
His nudity is a bit disgusting. Overmuscled
And a bit shameful, like an overdeveloped body-builder.
He has a juvenile look, a delinquent eye

Very unlikeable as he lifts his nostrils
And his upper lip, to test a newcomer.
Today none of that mooning around after cows,
That trundling obedience, like a trailer. None of the cows
Have any power today, and he's stopped looking.
He lays his head sideways, and worries the grass,
Keeping his intake steady.

15 September 1973

Sheep

I

The sheep has stopped crying.
All morning in her wire-mesh compound
On the lawn, she has been crying
For her vanished lamb. Yesterday they came.
Then her lamb could stand, in a fashion,
And make some tiptoe cringing steps.
Now he has disappeared.
He was only half the proper size.
And his cry was wrong. It was not
A dry little hard bleat, a baby-cry
Over a flat tongue, it was human,
It was a despairing human smooth Oh!
Like no lamb I ever heard. Its hindlegs
Cowered in under its lumped spine,
Its feeble hips leaned towards
Its shoulders for support. Its stubby
White wool pyramid head, on a tottery neck,
Had sad and defeated eyes, pinched, pathetic,
Too small, and it cried all the time
Oh! Oh! staggering towards
Its alert, baffled, stamping, storming mother
Who feared our intentions. He was too weak
To find her teats, or to nuzzle up in under,
He hadn't the gumption. He was fully
Occupied just standing, then shuffling
Towards where she'd removed to. She knew
He wasn't right, she couldn't
Make him out. Then his rough-curl legs,
So stoutly built, and hooved

With real quality tips,
Just got in the way, like a loose bundle
Of firewood he was cursed to manage,
Too heavy for him, lending sometimes
Some support, but no strength, no real help.
When we sat his mother on her tail, he mouthed her teat,
Slobbered a little, but after a minute
Lost aim and interest, his muzzle wandered,
He was managing a difficulty
Much more urgent and important. By evening
He could not stand. It was not
That he could not thrive, he was born
With everything but the will –
That can be deformed, just like a limb.
Death was more interesting to him.
Life could not get his attention.
So he died, with the yellow birth-mucus
Still in his cardigan.
He did not survive a warm summer night.
Now his mother has started crying again.
The wind is oceanic in the elms
And the blossom is all set.

20 May 1974

II

The mothers have come back
From the shearing, and behind the hedge
The woe of sheep is like a battlefield
In the evening, when the fighting is over,
And the cold begins, and the dew falls,
And bowed women move with water.

Mother Mother Mother the lambs
Are crying, and the mothers are crying.
Nothing can resist that probe, that cry
Of a lamb for its mother, or a ewe's crying
For its lamb. The lambs cannot find
Their mothers among those shorn strangers.
A half-hour they have lamented,
Shaking their voices in desperation.
Bald brutal-voiced mothers braying out,
Flat-tongued lambs chopping off hopelessness
Their hearts are in panic, their bodies
Are a mess of woe, woe they cry,
They mingle their trouble, a music
Of worse and worse distress, a worse entangling,
They hurry out little notes
With all their strength, cries searching this way and that.
The mothers force out sudden despair, blaaa!
On restless feet, with wild heads.

Their anguish goes on and on, in the June heat.
Only slowly their hurt dies, cry by cry,
As they fit themselves to what has happened.

   4 June 1976

The Lovepet

Was it an animal was it a bird?
She stroked it. He spoke to it softly.
She made her voice its happy forest.
He brought it out with sugarlump smiles.
Soon it was licking their kisses.

She gave it the strings of her voice which it swallowed
He gave it the blood of his face it grew eager
She gave it the liquorice of her mouth it began to thrive
He opened the aniseed of his future
And it bit and gulped, grew vicious, snatched
The focus of his eyes
She gave it the steadiness of her hand
He gave it the strength of his spine it ate everything

It began to cry what could they give it
They gave it their calendars it bolted their diaries
They gave it their sleep it gobbled their dreams
Even while they slept
It ate their bodyskin and the muscle beneath
They gave it vows its teeth clashed its starvation
Through every word they uttered

It found snakes under the floor it ate them
It found a spider horror
In their palms and ate it

They gave it double smiles and blank silence
It chewed holes in their carpets
They gave it logic
It ate the colour of their hair
They gave it every argument that would come

They gave it shouting and yelling they meant it
It ate the faces of their children
They gave it their photograph albums they gave it their
    records
It ate the colour of the sun
They gave it a thousand letters they gave it money
It ate their future complete it waited for them
Staring and starving
They gave it screams it had gone too far
It ate into their brains
It ate the roof
It ate lonely stone it ate wind crying famine
It went furiously off

They wept they called it back it could have everything
It stripped out their nerves chewed chewed flavourless
It bit at their numb bodies they did not resist
It bit into their blank brains they hardly knew

It moved bellowing
Through a ruin of starlight and crockery

It drew slowly off they could not move

It went far away they could not speak

Mosquito

To get into life
Mosquito died many deaths.

The slow millstone of polar ice, turned by the galaxy,
Only polished her egg.

Sub-zero, bulging all its mountain-power,
Failed to fracture her bubble.

The lake that squeezed her kneeled,
Tightened to granite – splintering quartz teeth,
But only sharpened her needle.

Till the strain was too much, even for Earth.

The stars drew off, trembling.
The mountains sat back, sweating.

The lake burst.

Mosquito

Flew up singing, over the broken waters –
A little haze of wings, a midget sun.

Cuckoo

Cuckoo's first cry, in light April,
Taps at the cool, suspended, ponderous jar
Of maiden blood
Like a finger-tip at a barometer.

That first ribald whoop, as a stolen kiss
Sets the diary trembling.
The orchard flushes. The hairy copse grows faint
With bluebells.

Sudden popping up of a lolling Priapus –
Hooha! Hooha!
Dizzying Milkymaids with innuendo.

Cuckoo jinks in – dowses his hawk-fright crucifix
Over the nest-bird's eye
And leaves his shadow in the egg.

Then his cry flees guilty – woodland to woodland,
Hunted by itself, all day dodging
The dropped double that dogs it.

O Orphan of Orphans! O moon-witted
Ill-bred dud-hawk!
Cavorting on pylons, you and your witchy moll!

With heartless blow on blow all afternoon
He opens hair-fine fractures through the heirloom
Chinaware hearts of spinsters in rose-cottages.

Then comes ducking under gates, pursued by a husband.
Or, invisibly, stately, through the blue shire
Trawls a vista-shimmering shawl of echo.

Later, the pair of them sit hiccoughing,
Chuckling, syncopating, translating
That lewd loopy shout

Into a ghoulish
Double-act, stuttering
Gag about baby-murder.

Swans

Washed in Arctic,
Return to their ballroom of glass
Still in the grip of the wizard,

With the jewel stuck in their throats.

Each one still condemned
To meditate all day on her mirror
Hypnotised with awe.

Each swan glued in her reflection
Airy
As the water-caught plume of a swan.

Each snowdrop lyrical daughter possessed
By the coil
Of a black and scowling serpent –

Dipping her eyes into subzero darkness,
Searching the dregs of old lakes
For her lost music.

Then they all writhe up the air,
A hard-hooved onset of cavalry –
Harp the iceberg wall with soft fingers.

Or drift, at evening, far out
Beyond islands, where the burning levels
Spill into the sun

And the snowflake of their enchantment melts.

Buzzard

Big hands, big thumbs, broad workaday hands
Darkened with working the land
Kneading the contours, squeezing out rats and rabbits.

Most of the day elongates a telephone pole
With his lighthouse lookout and swivel noddle.

O beggared eagle! O down-and-out falcon!
Mooning and ambling along hedgerow levels,
Forbidden the sun's glittering ascent –

As if you were sentenced to pick blackberries
At Easter, searching so fearful-careful,
So hopeless-careless, rag-wings, ragged trousers.

Too low-born for the peregrine's trapeze, too dopey
For the sparrowhawk's jet controls –
Where's the high dream when you rode circles

Mewing near the sun
Into your mirror-self – something unearthly
Lowering from heaven towards you?

Buzzard sits in mid-field, in mild sunlight,
Listening to tangled tales, by mole and by bee,
And by soft-headed dandelion.

When he treads, by chance, on a baby rabbit
He looks like an old woman
Trying to get her knickers off.

In the end he lumbers away
To find some other buzzard, maybe older,
To show him how.

Snipe

You are soaked with the cold rain –
Like a pelt in tanning liquor.
The moor's swollen waterbelly
Swags and quivers, ready to burst at a step.

Suddenly
Some scrap of dried fabric rips
Itself up
From the marsh-quake, scattering. A soft

Explosion of twilight
In the eyes, with a spinning fragment
Somewhere. Nearly lost, wing-flash

Stab-trying escape routes, wincing
From each, ducking under
And flinging up over –

Bowed head, jockey shoulders
Climbing headlong
As if hurled downwards –

A mote in the watery eye of the moor –

Hits cloud and
Skis down the far rain wall

Slashes a wet rent
In the rain-dusk
Twisting out sideways –

      rushes his alarm
Back to the ice-age.

The downpour helmet
Tightens on your skull, riddling the pools,
Washing the standing stones and fallen shales
With empty nightfall.

The Hen

The Hen
Worships the dust. She finds God everywhere.
Everywhere she finds his jewels.
And she does not care
What the cabbage thinks.

She has forgotten flight
Because she has interpreted happily
Her recurrent dream
Of clashing cleavers, of hot ovens,
And of the little pen-knife blade
Splitting her palate.
She flaps her wings, like shallow egg-baskets,
To show her contempt
For those who live on escape
And a future of empty sky.

She rakes, with noble, tireless foot,
The treasury of the dirt,
And clucks with the mechanical alarm clock
She chose instead of song
When the Creator
Separated the Workers and the Singers.

With her eye on reward
She tilts her head religiously
At the most practical angle
Which reveals to her
That the fox is a country superstition,
That her eggs have made man her slave
And that the heavens, for all their threatening,
Have not yet fallen.

And she is stern. Her eye is fierce – blood
(That weakness) is punished instantly.
She is a hard bronze of uprightness.
And indulges herself in nothing
Except to swoon a little, a delicious slight swoon,
One eye closed, just before sleep,
Conjuring the odour of tarragon.

Mallard

Gloom-glossy wind
Ransacking summer's end.

Crammed, churned leaf-mass.
The river's shutters clatter.

Myself mixed with it – gusty skeleton,
Scarecrow blown
Inside out, clinging to my straws –

Horizons rolling up. A space-witch
Mussel-blue, in a fling of foul skirts

Gapes a light-streak –

I squint up and vertigo
Has unbalanced the clouds, slithering everything

Into a sack.
                    As a dark horse – sudden
Little elf-horse – bolts for freedom.

Gallops out of the river
Flashes white chevrons, climbs

The avalanche of leaves, flickering pennons,
Whinnies overhead –
                    and is
Snatched away by a huge hand.

Evening Thrush

Beyond a twilight of limes and willows
The church craftsman is still busy –
Switing idols,
Rough pre-Goidelic gods and goddesses,
Out of old bits of churchyard yew.

Suddenly flinging
Everything off, head-up, flame-naked,
Plunges shuddering into the creator –

Then comes plodding back, with a limp, over cobbles.

That was a virtuoso's joke.

Now, serious, stretched full height, he aims
At the zenith. He situates a note
Right on the source of light.

Sews a seamless garment, simultaneously
Hurls javelins of dew
Three in air together, catches them.

Explains a studied theorem of sober practicality.

Cool-eyed,
Gossips in a mundane code of splutters
With Venus and Jupiter.
                              Listens –
Motionless, intent astronomer.

Suddenly launches a soul –

The first roses hang in a yoke stupor.
Globe after globe rolls out
Through his fluteful of dew –

The tree-stacks ride out on the widening arc.

Alone and darkening
At the altar of a star
With his sword through his throat
The thrush of clay goes on arguing
Over the graves.

O thrush,
If that really is you, behind the leaf-screen,
Who is this –

Worn-headed, on the lawn's grass, after sunset,
Humped, voiceless, turdus, imprisoned
As a long-distance lorry-driver, dazed

With the pop and static and unending
Of worms and wife and kids?

Treecreeper

On the tree-bole a zig-zag upward rivulet
Is a dodgy bird, a midget ace,
Busy as a shrew, moth-modest as lichen.

Inchmeal medical examination
Of the tree's skin. Snap-shot micro-scanner
And a bill of instant hypodermic.

He's unzipping the tree-bole
For deeper scrutiny. It sticks. It jerks.
No microbe dare be, nor bubble spider.

All the trees are waiting – pale, undressed –
So he can't dawdle. He jabs, dabs, checks essentials,
Magnet-safe on undersides, then swings

In a blur of tiny machinery
To the next patient's foot, and trickles upward
Murmuring 'Good, good!' and 'Good, good!'

Into the huge satisfying mass of work.

A Dove

Snaps its twig-tether – mounts –
Dream-yanked up into vacuum
Wings snickering.

Another, in a shatter, hurls dodging away up.

They career through tree-mazes –
Nearly uncontrollable love-weights.

Or now
Temple-dancers, possessed, and steered
By solemn powers
Through insane, stately convulsions.

Porpoises
Of dove-lust and blood splendour
With arcs
And plungings, and spray-slow explosions.

Now violently gone
Riding the snake of the long love-whip
Among flarings of mares and stallions

Now staying
Coiled on a bough
Bubbling molten, wobbling top-heavy
Into one and many.

Sing the Rat

Sing the hole's plume, the rafter's cockade
Who melts from the eye-corner, the soft squealer
Pointed at both ends, who chews through lead

Sing the scholarly meek face
Of the penniless rat
Who studies all night
To inherit the house

Sing the riff-raff of the roof-space, who dance till dawn
Sluts in silk, sharpers with sleek moustaches
Dancing the cog-roll, the belly-bounce, the trundle

Sing the tireless hands
Of the hardworking rat
Who demolishes the crust, and does not fail
To sign the spilt flour

The rat, the rat, the ratatatat
The house's poltergeist, shaped like a shuttle
Who longs to join the family

Sing his bright face, cross-eyed with eagerness
His pin-fingers, that seem too small for the job
Sing his split nose, that looks so sore
O sing his fearless ears, the listener in the wall

Let him jump on your head, let him cling there
Save him from sticks and stones

Sing the rat so poor he thrives on poison
Who has nothing to give to the trap, though it gapes for
    a year
Except his children

Who prays only to the ferret
'Forget me' and to the terrier
'In every thousand of me, spare two'

Sing him

Who stuffs his velvet purse, in hurry and fear
With the memory of the fork,
The reflections of the spoon, the hope of the knives

Who woos his wife with caperings, who thinks deep

Who is the slave of two fangs

O sing
The long-tailed grey worry of the night-hours
Who always watches and waits
Like a wart on the nose
Even while you snore

O sing
Little Jesus in the wilderness
Carrying the sins of the house
Into every dish, the hated one

O sing
Scupper-tyke, whip-lobber
Smutty-guts, pot-goblin
Garret-whacker, rick-lark
Sump-swab, cupboard-adder
Bobby-robin, knacker-knocker
Sneak-nicker, sprinty-dinty
Pintle-bum

Swallows

What The Schoolmaster Said:

She flicks past, ahead of her name,
Twinkling away out over the lake.

Reaching this way and that way, with her scissors,
Snipping midges
Trout are too numb and sunken to stir for.

Sahara clay ovens, at mirage heat,
Glazed her blues, and still she is hot.

She wearied of snatching clegs off the lugs of buffaloes
And of lassooing the flirt-flags of gazelles.

They told her the North was one giant snowball
Rolling South. She did not believe them.
She exchanged the starry chart of Columbus
For a beggar's bowl of mud.

Did she close her eyes and trust in God?
No, she saw lighthouses
Streaming in chaos
Like sparks from a chymney –

She had fixed her instruments on home.

So now, suddenly, into a blanch-tree stillness,
A silence of celandines,
A fringing and stupor of frost
She bursts, weightless –
                            and anchors
On eggs frail as frost.

There she goes, flung taut on her leash,
Her eyes at her mouth-corners,

Water-skiing out across a wind
That wrecks great flakes against windscreens.

What The Farmer's Wife Said:

It's the loveliest thing about swallows,
The moment they come,
The moment they dip in, and are suddenly there.

For months you just never thought about them
Then suddenly you see one swimming maybe out there
Over our bare tossing orchard, in a slattery April blow,
Probably among big sloppy snowflakes.

And there it is – the first swallow,
Flung and frail, like a midge caught in the waterskin
On the weir's brink – and straightaway you lose it.
You just got a glimpse of whisker and frailty

Then there's nothing but jostled daffodils, like the girls
        running in from a downpour
Shrieking and giggling and shivering
And the puckered primrose posies, and the wet grit.
It's only a moment, only a flicker, easy to miss –

That first swallow just swinging in your eye-corner
Like a mote in the wind-smart,
A swallow pinned on a roller of air that roars and
        snatches it away

Out of sight, and booms in the bare wood

And you know there'll be colder nights yet
And worse days and you think
'If he's here, there must be flies for him'
And you think of the flies and their thin limbs in that cold.

What The Vicar Said:

I agree
There's nothing verminous, or pestilential, about swallows.
Swallows are the aristocrats
The thoroughbreds of summer.
Still, there is something sinister about them.
I think it's their futuristic design.
The whole evolution of aircraft
Has been to resemble swallows more and more closely.
None of that propellor-blur, ponderous, biplane business
Of partridges and pheasants,
Or even the spitfire heroics of hawks.
When I was a boy I remember
Their shapes always alarmed me, slightly,
With the thought of the wars to come,
The speed beyond sound, the molten forms.
You might say
They have a chirruppy, chicken-sweet expression
With goo-goo starlet wide-apart eyes,
And their bills seem tiny, almost retroussé cute –
In fact, the whole face opens
Like a jet engine.

And before this, they solved the problem, did they not,
Of the harpoon.

Under the Hill of Centurions

The river is in a resurrection fever.
Now at Easter you find them
Up in the pool's throat, and in the very jugular
Where the stickle pulses under grasses –

Cock minnows!

They have abandoned contemplation and prayer in the
    pool's crypt.

There they are, packed all together,
In an inch of seething light.

A stag-party, all bridegrooms, all in their panoply –

Red-breasted as if they bled, their Roman
Bottle-glass greened bodies silked with black

In the clatter of the light loom of water
All singing and
Toiling together,
Wreathing their metals
Into the warp and weft of the lit water –

I imagine their song,
Deep-chested, striving, solemn.

A wrestling tress of kingfisher colour,
Steely jostlings, a washed mass of brilliants

Labouring at earth
In the wheel of light –

Ghostly rinsings
A struggle of spirits.

Milesian Encounter on the Sligachan

for Hilary and Simon

'Up in the pools,' they'd said, and 'Two miles upstream.'

Something sinister about bogland rivers.

And a shock –

after the two miles of tumblequag, of Ice-Age hairiness,
crusty, quaking cadaver and me lurching over it in elation
like a daddy-long-legs –

after crooked little clatterbrook and again clatterbrook (a
hurry of shallow grey light so distilled it looked like acid) –

and after the wobbly levels of a razor-edged, blood-smeared
grass, the flood-sucked swabs of bog-cotton, the dusty calico
rip-up of snipe –

under those petrified scapulae, vertebrae, horn-skulls the
Cuillins (asylum of eagles) that were blue-silvered like
wrinkled baking foil in the blue noon that day, and
tremulous –

early August, in a hot lateness (only three hours before my
boat), a glimpse of my watch and suddenly

up to my hip in a suck-hole then on again teetering over the
broken-necked heath-bobs a good half-hour and me melting
in my combined fuel of toil and clobber suddenly

The shock.
The sheer cavern of current piling silence
Under my feet.

So lonely-drowning deep, so drowned-hair silent

So clear
Cleansing the body cavity of the underbog.

Such a brilliant cut-glass interior
Sliding under me

And I felt a little bit giddy
Ghostly
As I fished the long pool-tail
Peering into that superabundance of spirit.

And now where were they, my fellow aliens from prehistory?
Those peculiar eyes
So like mine, but fixed at zero,
Pressing in from outer darkness
Eyes of aimed sperm and of egg on their errand,
Looking for immortality
In the lap of a broken volcano, in the furrow of a lost glacier,
Those shuttles of love-shadow?

Only humbler beings waved at me –
Weeds grazing the bottom, idling their tails.

Till the last pool –
A broad, coiling whorl, a deep ear
Of pondering amber,
Greenish and precious like a preservative,
With a ram's skull sunk there – magnified, a Medusa,
Funereal, phosphorescent, a lamp
Ten feet under the whisky.

I heard this pool whisper a warning.

I tickled its leading edges with temptation.
I stroked its throat with a whisker.
I licked the moulded hollows

Of its collarbones
Where the depth, now underbank opposite,
Pulsed up from contained excitements –

Eerie how you know when it's coming –
So I felt it now, my blood
Prickling and thickening, altering
With an ushering-in of chills, a weird onset
As if mountains were pushing mountains higher
Behind me, to crowd over my shoulder –

Then the pool lifted a travelling bulge
And grabbed the tip of my heart-nerve, and crashed,

Trying to wrench it from me, and again
Lifted a flash of arm for leverage
And it was a Gruagach of the Sligachan!
Some Boggart up from a crack in the granite!
A Glaistig out of the skull!
                                        – what was it gave me
Such a supernatural, beautiful fright

And let go, and sank disembodied
Into the eye-pupil darkness?

Only a little salmon.
                    Salmo salar
The loveliest, left-behind, most-longed-for ogress
Of the Palaeolithic
Watched me through her time-warped judas-hole
In the ruinous castle of Skye

As I faded from the light of reality.

That Morning

We came where the salmon were so many
So steady, so spaced, so far-aimed
On their inner map, England could add

Only the sooty twilight of South Yorkshire
Hung with the drumming drift of Lancasters
Till the world had seemed capsizing slowly.

Solemn to stand there in the pollen light
Waist-deep in wild salmon swaying massed
As from the hand of God. There the body

Separated, golden and imperishable,
From its doubting thought – a spirit-beacon
Lit by the power of the salmon

That came on, came on, and kept on coming
As if we flew slowly, their formations
Lifting us toward some dazzle of blessing

One wrong thought might darken. As if the fallen
World and salmon were over. As if these
Were the imperishable fish

That had let the world pass away –

There, in a mauve light of drifted lupins,
They hung in the cupped hands of mountains

Made of tingling atoms. It had happened.
Then for a sign that we were where we were
Two gold bears came down and swam like men

Beside us. And dived like children.
And stood in deep water as on a throne
Eating pierced salmon off their talons.

So we found the end of our journey.

So we stood, alive in the river of light
Among the creatures of light, creatures of light.

A Rival

The cormorant, commissar of the hard sea,
Has not adjusted to the soft river.

He lifts his pterodactyl head in the drought pool
(Sound-proof cellar of final solutions).

The dinosaur massacre-machine
Hums on in his skull, programme unaltered.

That fossil eye-chip could reduce
All the blood in the world, yet still taste nothing.

At dawn he's at it, under the sick face –
Cancer in the lymph, uncontrollable.

Level your eye's aim and he's off
Knocking things over, out through the window –

An abortion-doctor
Black bag packed with vital organs

Dripping unspeakably.
                    Then away, heavy, high
Over the sea's iron curtain –

The pool lies there mutilated,
                        face averted,
Dumb and ruined.

Performance

Just before the curtain falls in the river
The Damselfly, with offstage, inaudible shriek
Reappears, weightless.

Hover-poised, in her snake-skin leotards,
Her violet-dark elegance.

Eyelash-delicate, a dracula beauty,
In her acetylene jewels.

Her mascara smudged, her veils shimmer-fresh –

Late August. Some sycamore leaves
Already in their museum, eaten to lace.
Robin song bronze-touching the stillness
Over posthumous nettles. The swifts, as one,
Whipcracked, gone. Blackberries.
                                And now, lightly,
Adder-shock of this dainty assassin
Still in mid-passion –
                        still in her miracle play:
Masked, archaic, mute, insect mystery
Out of the sun's crypt.
                        Everything is forgiven
Such a metamorphosis in love!
Phaedra Titania
Dragon of crazed enamels!
Tragedienne of the ultra-violet,
So sulphurous and so frail,

Stepping so magnetically to her doom!

Lifted out of the river with tweezers

Dripping the sun's incandescence –
                              suddenly she
Switches her scene elsewhere.

    (Find him later, halfway up a nettle,
    A touch-crumple petal of web and dew –

    Midget puppet-clown, tranced on his strings,
    In the nightfall pall of balsam.)

An Eel

The strange part is his head. Her head. The strangely ripened
Domes over the brain, swollen nacelles
For some large containment. Lobed glands
Of some large awareness. Eerie the eel's head.
This full, plum-sleeked fruit of evolution.
Beneath it, her snout's a squashed slipper-face,
The mouth grin-long and perfunctory,
Undershot predatory. And the iris, dirty gold
Distilled only enough to be different
From the olive lode of her body,
The grained and woven blacks. And ringed larger
With a vaguer vision, an earlier eye
Behind her eye, paler, blinder,
Inward. Her buffalo hump
Begins the amazement of her progress.
Her mid-shoulder pectoral fin – concession
To fish-life – secretes itself
Flush with her concealing suit: under it
The skin's a pale exposure of deepest eel
As her belly is, a dulled pearl.
Strangest, the thumb-print skin, the rubberised weave
Of her insulation. Her whole body
Damascened with identity. This is she
Suspends the Sargasso
In her inmost hope. Her life is a cell
Sealed from event, her patience
Global and furthered with love
By the bending stars as if she
Were earth's sole initiate. Alone

In her millions, the moon's pilgrim,
The nun of water.

II

Where does the river come from?
And the eel, the night-mind of water –
The river within the river and opposite –
The night-nerve of water?

Not from the earth's remembering mire
Not from the air's whim
Not from the brimming sun. Where from?

From the bottom of the nothing pool
Sargasso of God
Out of the empty spiral of stars

A glimmering person

October Salmon

He's lying in poor water, a yard or so depth of poor safety,
Maybe only two feet under the no-protection of an outleaning
    small oak,
Half under a tangle of brambles.

After his two thousand miles, he rests,
Breathing in that lap of easy current
In his graveyard pool.

About six pounds weight,
Four years old at most, and hardly a winter at sea –
But already a veteran,
Already a death-patched hero. So quickly it's over!

So briefly he roamed the gallery of marvels!
Such sweet months, so richly embroidered into earth's
    beauty-dress,
Her life-robe –
Now worn out with her tirelessness, her insatiable quest,
Hangs in the flow, a frayed scarf –

An autumnal pod of his flower,
The mere hull of his prime, shrunk at shoulder and flank,

With the sea-going Aurora Borealis
Of his April power –
The primrose and violet of that first upfling in the estuary –
Ripened to muddy dregs,
The river reclaiming his sea-metals.

In the October light
He hangs there, patched with leper-cloths.

Death has already dressed him
In her clownish regimentals, her badges and decorations,
Mapping the completion of his service,
His face a ghoul-mask, a dinosaur of senility, and his whole
    body
A fungoid anemone of canker –

Can the caress of water ease him?
The flow will not let up for a minute.

What a change! from that covenant of polar light
To this shroud in a gutter!
What a death-in-life – to be his own spectre!
His living body become death's puppet,
Dolled by death in her crude paints and drapes
He haunts his own staring vigil
And suffers the subjection, and the dumbness,
And the humiliation of the role!

And that is how it is,
That is what is going on there, under the scrubby oak tree,
    hour after hour,
That is what the splendour of the sea has come down to,
And the eye of ravenous joy – king of infinite liberty
In the flashing expanse, the bloom of sea-life,

On the surge-ride of energy, weightless,
Body simply the armature of energy
In that earliest sea-freedom, the savage amazement of life,
The salt mouthful of actual existence
With strength like light –

Yet this was always with him. This was inscribed in his egg.
This chamber of horrors is also home.
He was probably hatched in this very pool.

And this was the only mother he ever had, this uneasy channel
      of minnows
Under the mill-wall, with bicycle wheels, car-tyres, bottles
And sunk sheets of corrugated iron.
People walking their dogs trail their evening shadows across him.
If boys see him they will try to kill him.

All this, too, is stitched into the torn richness,
The epic poise
That holds him so steady in his wounds, so loyal to his doom,
      so patient
In the machinery of heaven.

Visitation

All night the river's twists
Bit each other's tails, in happy play.

Suddenly a dark other
Twisted among them.

And a cry, half sky, half bird,
Slithered over roots.
                         A star
Fleetingly etched it.
                         Dawn
Puzzles a sunk branch under deep tremblings.

Nettles will not tell.
                    Who shall say
That the river
Crawled out of the river, and whistled,
And was answered by another river?

A strange tree
Is the water of life –

Sheds these pad-clusters on mud-margins
One dawn in a year, her eeriest flower.

The Hare

I

That Elf
Riding his awkward pair of haunchy legs

That weird long-eared Elf
Wobbling down the highway

Don't overtake him, don't try to drive past him,
He's scatty, he's all over the road,
He can't keep his steering, in his ramshackle go-cart,
His big loose wheels, buckled and rusty,
Nearly wobbling off

And all the screws in his head wobbling and loose

And his eyes wobbling

II

The Hare is a very fragile thing.
The life in the hare is a glassy goblet, and her yellow-
    fringed frost-flake belly says: Fragile.

The hare's bones are light glass. And the hare's face –

Who lifted her face to the Lord?
Her new-budded nostrils and lips,
For the daintiest pencillings, the last eyelash touches

Delicate as the down of a moth,
And the breath of awe
Which fixed the mad beauty-light
In her look

As if her retina
Were a moon perpetually at full.

Who is it, at midnight on the A30,
The Druid soul,
The night-streaker, the sudden lumpy goblin
That thumps your car under the belly
Then cries with human pain
And becomes a human baby on the road
That you dare hardly pick up?

Or leaps, like a long bat with little headlights,
Straight out of darkness
Into the driver's nerves
With a jangle of cries
As if the car had crashed into a flying harp

So that the driver's nerves flail and cry
Like a burst harp.

III

Uneasy she nears
As if she were being lured, but fearful,
Nearer.
Like a large egg toppling itself – mysterious!

Then she'll stretch, tall, on her hind feet,
And lean on the air,
Taut – like a stilled yacht waiting on the air –

And what does the hunter see? A fairy woman?
A dream beast?
A kangaroo of the March corn?

The loveliest face listening,
Her black-tipped ears hearing the bud of the blackthorn

Opening its lips,
Her black-tipped hairs hearing tomorrow's weather
Combing the mare's tails,
Her snow-fluff belly feeling for the first breath,
Her orange nape, foxy with its dreams of the fox –

Witch-maiden
Heavy with trembling blood – astounding
How much blood there is in her body!
She is a moony pond of quaking blood

Twitched with spells, her gold-ringed eye spellbound –

Carrying herself so gently, balancing
Herself with the gentlest touches
As if her eyes brimmed –

Two Tortoiseshell Butterflies

Mid-May – after May frosts that killed the Camellias,
After May snow. After a winter
Worst in human memory, a freeze
Killing the hundred-year-old Bay Tree,
And the ten-year-old Bay Tree – suddenly
A warm limpness. A blue heaven just veiled
With the sweatings of earth
And with the sweatings-out of winter
Feverish under the piled
Maywear of the lawn.
              Now two
Tortoiseshell butterflies, finding themselves alive,
She drunk with the earth-sweat, and he
Drunk with her, float in eddies
Over the Daisies' quilt. She prefers Dandelions,
Settling to nod her long spring tongue down
Into the nestling pleats, into the flower's
Thick-folded throat, her wings high-folded.
He settling behind her, among plain glistenings
Of the new grass, edging and twitching
To nearly touch – pulsing and convulsing
Wings wide open to tight-closed to flat open
Quivering to keep her so near, almost reaching
To stroke her abdomen with his antennae –
Then she's up and away, and he startlingly
Swallowlike overtaking, crowding her, heading her
Off any escape. She turns that
To her purpose, and veers down
Onto another Dandelion, attaching
Her weightless yacht to its crest.

Wobbles to stronger hold, to deeper, sweeter
Penetration, her wings tight shut above her,
A sealed book, absorbed in itself.
She ignores him
Where he edges to left and to right, flitting
His wings open, titillating her fur
With his perfumed draughts, spasming his patterns,
His tropical, pheasant appeals of folk-art,
Venturing closer, grass-blade by grass-blade,
Trembling with inhibition, nearly touching –
And again she's away, dithering blackly. He swoops
On an elastic to settle accurately
Under her tail again as she clamps to
This time a Daisy. She's been chosen,
Courtship has claimed her. And he's been conscripted
To what's required
Of the splitting bud, of the talented robin
That performs piercings
Out of the still-bare ash,
The whole air just like him, just breathing
Over the still-turned-inward earth, the first
Caresses of the wedding coming, the earth
Opening its petals, the whole sky
Opening a flower
Of unfathomably-patterned pollen.

In the Likeness of a Grasshopper

A trap
Waits on the field path.

A wicker contraption, with working parts,
Its spring tensed and set.

So flimsily made, out of grass
(Out of the stems, the joints, the raspy-dry flags).

Baited with a fur-soft caterpillar,
A belly of amorous life, pulsing signals.

Along comes a love-sick, perfume-footed
Music of the wild earth.

The trap, touched by a breath,
Jars into action, its parts blur –

And music cries out.

A sinewy violin
Has caught its violinist.

Cloud-fingered summer, the beautiful trapper,
Picks up the singing cage

And takes out the Song, adds it to the Songs
With which she robes herself, which are her wealth,

Sets her trap again, a yard further on.

A Sparrow Hawk

Slips from your eye-corner – overtaking
Your first thought.

Through your mulling gaze over haphazard earth
The sun's cooled carbon wing
Whets the eyebeam.

Those eyes in their helmet
Still wired direct
To the nuclear core – they alone

Laser the lark-shaped hole
In the lark's song.

You find the fallen spurs, among soft ashes.

And maybe you find him

Materialised by twilight and dew
Still as a listener –

The warrior

Blue shoulder-cloak wrapped about him
Leaning, hunched,
Among the oaks of the harp.

Wolfwatching

Woolly-bear white, the old wolf
Is listening to London. His eyes, withered in
Under the white wool, black peepers,
While he makes nudging, sniffing offers
At the horizon of noise, the blue-cold April
Invitation of airs. The lump of meat
Is his confinement. He has probably had all his life
Behind wires, fraying his eye-efforts
On the criss-cross embargo. He yawns
Peevishly like an old man and the yawn goes
Right back into Kensington and there stops
Floored with glaze. Eyes
Have worn him away. Children's gazings
Have tattered him to a lumpish
Comfort of woolly play-wolf. He's weary.
He curls on the cooling stone
That gets heavier. Then again the burden
Of a new curiosity, a new testing
Of new noises, new people with new colours
Are coming in at the gate. He lifts
The useless weight and lets it sink back,
Stirring and settling in a ball of unease.
All his power is a tangle of old ends,
A jumble of leftover scraps and bits of energy
And bitten-off impulses and dismantled intuitions.
He can't settle. He's ruffling
And re-organizing his position all day
Like a sleepless half-sleep of growing agonies
In a freezing car. The day won't pass.
The night will be worse. He's waiting

For the anaesthetic to work
That has already taken his strength, his beauty
And his life.

He levers his stiffness erect
And angles a few tottering steps
Into his habits. He goes down to water
And drinks. Age is thirsty. Water
Just might help and ease. What else
Is there to do? He tries to find again
That warm position he had. He cowers
His hind legs to curl under him. Subsides
In a trembling of wolf-pelt he no longer
Knows how to live up to.
                                    And here
Is a young wolf, still intact.
He knows how to lie, with his head,
The Asiatic eyes, the gunsights
Aligned effortless in the beam of his power.
He closes his pale eyes and is easy,
Bored easy. His big limbs
Are full of easy time. He's waiting
For the chance to live, then he'll be off.
Meanwhile the fence, and the shadow-flutter
Of moving people, and the roller-coaster
Roar of London surrounding, are temporary,
And cost him nothing, and he can afford
To prick his ears to all that and find nothing
As to forest. He still has the starlings
To amuse him. The scorched ancestries,
Grizzled into his back, are his royalty.
The rufous ears and neck are always ready.
He flops his heavy running paws, resplays them

On pebbles, and rests the huge engine
Of his purring head. A wolf
Dropped perfect on pebbles. For eyes
To put on a pedestal. A product
Without a market.
                            But all the time
The awful thing is happening: the iron inheritance,
The incredibly rich will, torn up
In neurotic boredom and eaten,
Now indigestible. All that restlessness
And lifting of ears, and aiming, and re-aiming
Of nose, is like a trembling
Of nervous breakdown, afflicted by voices.
Is he hearing the deer? Is he listening
To gossip of non-existent forest? Pestered
By the hour-glass panic of lemmings
Dwindling out of reach? He's run a long way
Now to find nothing and be patient.
Patience is suffocating in all those folds
Of deep fur. The fairy tales
Grow stale all around him
And go back into pebbles. His eyes
Keep telling him all this is real
And that he's a wolf – of all things
To be in the middle of London, of all
Futile, hopeless things. Do Arctics
Whisper on their wave-lengths – fantasy-draughts
Of escape and freedom? His feet,
The power-tools, lie in front of him –
He doesn't know how to use them. Sudden
Dramatic lift and re-alignment
Of his purposeful body –

                                    the Keeper
Has come to freshen the water.

And the prodigious journeys
Are thrown down again in his
Loose heaps of rope.
The future's snapped and coiled back
Into a tangled lump, a whacking blow
That's damaged his brain. Quiet,
Amiable in his dogginess,
Disillusioned – all that preparation
Souring in his skin. His every yawn
Is another dose of poison. His every frolic
Releases a whole flood
Of new hopelessness which he then
Has to burn up in sleep. A million miles
Knotted in his paws. Ten million years
Broken between his teeth. A world
Stinking on the bone, pecked by sparrows.

He's hanging
Upside down on the wire
Of non-participation.
He's a tarot-card, and he knows it.
He can howl all night
And dawn will pick up the same card
And see him painted on it, with eyes
Like doorframes in a desert
Between nothing and nothing.

from Arachne

Minerva tore from the loom
That gallery of divine indiscretions
And ripped it to rags.
Then, all her power gone
Into exasperation, struck Arachne

With her boxwood shuttle
One blow between the eyes, then another,
Then a third, and a fourth. Arachne
Staggered away groaning with indignation.
She refused to live

With the injustice. Making a noose
And fitting it round her neck
She jumped into air, jerked at the rope's end,
And dangled, and spun.
Pity touched Minerva.

She caught the swinging girl: 'You have been wicked
Enough to dangle there for ever
And so you shall. But alive,
And your whole tribe the same through all time
Populating the earth.'

The goddess
Squeezed onto the dangling Arachne
Venom from Hecate's deadliest leaf.
Under that styptic drop
The poor girl's head shrank to a poppy seed

And her hair fell out.
Her eyes, her ears, her nostrils
Diminished beyond being. Her body

Became a tiny ball.
And now she is all belly

With a dot of head. She retains
Only her slender skilful fingers
For legs. And so for ever
She hangs from the thread that she spins
Out of her belly.

Or ceaselessly weaves it
Into patterned webs
On a loom of leaves and grasses –
Her touches
Deft and swift and light as when they were human.

The Owl

I saw my world again through your eyes
As I would see it again through your children's eyes.
Through your eyes it was foreign.
Plain hedge hawthorns were peculiar aliens,
A mystery of peculiar lore and doings.
Anything wild, on legs, in your eyes
Emerged at a point of exclamation
As if it had appeared to dinner guests
In the middle of the table. Common mallards
Were artefacts of some unearthliness,
Their wooings were a hypnagogic film
Unreeled by the river. Impossible
To comprehend the comfort of their feet
In the freezing water. You were a camera
Recording reflections you could not fathom.
I made my world perform its utmost for you.
You took it all in with an incredulous joy
Like a mother handed her new baby
By the midwife. Your frenzy made me giddy.
It woke up my dumb, ecstatic boyhood
Of fifteen years before. My masterpiece
Came that black night on the Grantchester road.
I sucked the throaty thin woe of a rabbit
Out of my wetted knuckle, by a copse
Where a tawny owl was enquiring.
Suddenly it swooped up, splaying its pinions
Into my face, taking me for a post.

The Chipmunk

A rippling, bobbing wood-elf, the chipmunk came
Under the Cape Cod conifers, over roots,
A first scout of the continent's wild game,
Midget aboriginal American. Flowing
On electrical accurate feet
Through its circuitry. That was the first real native –
Dodging from flashlit listening still
To staring flashlit still. It studied me
Sitting at a book – a strange prisoner,
Pacing my priceless years away, eyes lowered,
To and fro, to and fro,
Across my page. It snapped a tail-gesture at me –
Roused me, peremptory, to this friendship
It would be sharing with me
Only a few more seconds.
                              Its eyes
Popping with inky joy,
Globed me in a new vision, woke me,
And I recognised it.
                         You stayed
Alien to me as a window model,
American, airport-hopping superproduct,
Through all our intimate weeks up to the moment,
In a flash-still, retorting to my something,
You made a chipmunk face. I thought
An eight-year-old child was suddenly a chipmunk.
Pursed mouth, puffed cheeks. And suddenly,
Just in that flash – as I laughed
And got my snapshot for life,
And shouted: 'That's my first ever real chipmunk!' –
A ghost, dim, a woodland spirit, swore me
To take his orphan.

Epiphany

London. The grimy lilac softness
Of an April evening. Me
Walking over Chalk Farm Bridge
On my way to the tube station.
A new father – slightly light-headed
With the lack of sleep and the novelty.
Next, this young fellow coming towards me.

I glanced at him for the first time as I passed him
Because I noticed (I couldn't believe it)
What I'd been ignoring.

Not the bulge of a small animal
Buttoned into the top of his jacket
The way colliers used to wear their whippets –
But its actual face. Eyes reaching out
Trying to catch my eyes – so familiar!
The huge ears, the pinched, urchin expression –
The wild confronting stare, pushed through fear,
Between the jacket lapels.
                              'It's a fox-cub!'
I heard my own surprise as I stopped.
He stopped. 'Where did you get it? What
Are you going to do with it?'
                              A fox-cub
On the hump of Chalk Farm Bridge!

'You can have him for a pound.' 'But
Where did you find it? What will you do with it?'
'Oh, somebody'll buy him. Cheap enough
At a pound.' And a grin.
                              What I was thinking

Was – what would you think? How would we fit it
Into our crate of space? With the baby?
What would you make of its old smell
And its mannerless energy?
And as it grew up and began to enjoy itself
What would we do with an unpredictable,
Powerful, bounding fox?
The long-mouthed, flashing temperament?
That necessary nightly twenty miles
And that vast hunger for everything beyond us?
How would we cope with its cosmic derangements
Whenever we moved?

The little fox peered past me at other folks,
At this one and at that one, then at me.
Good luck was all it needed.
Already past the kittenish
But the eyes still small,
Round, orphaned-looking, woebegone
As if with weeping. Bereft
Of the blue milk, the toys of feather and fur,
The den life's happy dark. And the huge whisper
Of the constellations
Out of which Mother had always returned.
My thoughts felt like big, ignorant hounds
Circling and sniffing around him.
                                        Then I walked on
As if out of my own life.
I let that fox-cub go. I tossed it back
Into the future
Of a fox-cub in London and I hurried
Straight on and dived as if escaping
Into the Underground. If I had paid,

If I had paid that pound and turned back
To you, with that armful of fox –

If I had grasped that whatever comes with a fox
Is what tests a marriage and proves it a marriage –
I would not have failed the test. Would you have failed it?
But I failed. Our marriage had failed.

from The Boy Changed into a Stag
Cries Out at the Gate of Secrets

Come back, my own son, come back
 for I am no longer as I was,
 I am a used-up shadow from the inner visions
 that flare through the thickening organs
 like an old cock's crowing, on winter dawns,
from a fence of shirts hanging board-frozen.
I am calling, your own mother,
come back, my own son, come back,
force new order onto the anarchic things,
discipline the savage objects, tame the knife and domesticate
 the comb,
because now I am only two gritty green eyes
glassy and weightless, like the dragonfly,
whose winged nape and mouth, that you know so well, so
 delicately clasp
two crystal apples in the green-illumined skull,
I am two staring eyes without a face,
seeing all, and one with the unearthly beings.
Come back, my own son, come back into place,
 with your fresh breath bring everything again to
 order.

 In the remote forest the boy heard.
 He jerked up his head in an instant,
 his spread nostrils testing the air,
 his soft dewlap throbbing, the veined ears pointing
 tautly to that lamenting music
 as to the still tread of the hunter,
 as to hot wisps fronding from the cradle
 of a forest fire, when the skyline trees

smoke and begin to whimper bluely.
He turned his head to the old voice,
and now an agony fastens on him,
and he sees the shag hair over his buttocks,
and he sees, on his bony legs,
the cleft hooves that deal his track,
sees, where lilies look up in pools,
low-slung hair-pursed buck-balls.
He forces his way towards the lake,
crashing the brittle willow thickets,
haunches plastered with foam that spatters
to the earth at his every bound,
his four black hooves rip him a path
through a slaughter of wild flowers,
sock a lizard into the mud,
throat ballooned and tail sheared,
till he reaches the lake at last,
and looks in at its lit window
that holds the moon, moving beech-boughs,
and a stag staring at him.
For the first time he sees the bristling pelt
covering all his lean body,
hair over knees and thighs, the transverse
tasselled lips of his male purse,
his long skull treed with antlers,
bone boughs bursting to bone leaves,
his face closely furred to the chin,
his nostrils slit and slanted in.
The great antlers knock against trees,
roped veins lump on his neck,
he strains fiercely, stamping he tries
to put out an answering cry, but in vain,
it is only a stag's voice belling

in the throat of this mother's son,
and he scatters a son's tears, trampling the shallows
to drive out that lake-horror, scare it
down into the whirlpool gullet
of the water-dark, where glittering
little fishes flicker their laces,
miniature bubble-eyed jewellery.
The ripples smooth off into the gloom,
but still a stag stands in the foam of the moon.

after the Hungarian by FERENC JUHÁSZ

The Prophet

Crazed by my soul's thirst
Through a dark land I staggered.
And a six-winged seraph
Halted me at a crossroads.
With fingers of dream
He touched my eye-pupils.
My eyes, prophetic, recoiled
Like a startled eaglet's.
He touched my ears
And a thunderous clangour filled them,
The shudderings of heaven,
The huge wingbeat of angels,
The submarine migration of sea-reptiles
And the burgeoning of the earth's vine.
He forced my mouth wide,
Plucked out my own cunning
Garrulous evil tongue,
And with bloody fingers
Between by frozen lips
Inserted the fork of a wise serpent.
He split my chest with a blade,
Wrenched my heart from its hiding,
And into the open wound
Dropped a flaming coal.
I lay on stones like a corpse.
There God's voice came to me:
'Stand, Prophet, you are my will.
Be my witness. Go
Through all seas and lands. With the Word
Burn the hearts of the people.'

after the Russian by ALEXANDER PUSHKIN

[170]

The Prophet

Crazed by my soul's thirst
Through a dark land I staggered.
And a six-winged seraph
Halted me at a crossroads.
With fingers of dream
He touched my eye-pupils.
My eyes, prophetic, recoiled
Like a startled eaglet's.
He touched my ears
And a thunderous clangour filled them,
The shudderings of heaven,
The huge wingbeat of angels,
The submarine migration of sea-reptiles
And the burgeoning of the earth's vine.
He forced my mouth wide,
Plucked out my own cunning
Garrulous evil tongue,
And with bloody fingers
Between by frozen lips
Inserted the fork of a wise serpent.
He split my chest with a blade,
Wrenched my heart from its hiding,
And into the open wound
Dropped a flaming coal.
I lay on stones like a corpse.
There God's voice came to me:
'Stand, Prophet, you are my will.
Be my witness. Go
Through all seas and lands. With the Word
Burn the hearts of the people.'

after the Russian by ALEXANDER PUSHKIN

[170]

in the throat of this mother's son,
and he scatters a son's tears, trampling the shallows
to drive out that lake-horror, scare it
down into the whirlpool gullet
of the water-dark, where glittering
little fishes flicker their laces,
miniature bubble-eyed jewellery.
The ripples smooth off into the gloom,
but still a stag stands in the foam of the moon.

after the Hungarian by FERENC JUHÁSZ